HOW TO STOP
THE BATTLE
WITH YOUR CHILD

A Practical Guide to Solving
Everyday Problems with Children

DON FLEMING, Ph.D.
with Linda Balahoutis
Illustrations by Bill Melendez

A FIRESIDE BOOK
Published by Simon & Schuster
New York London Toronto Sydney Tokyo Singapore

FIRESIDE

Rockefeller Center
1230 Avenue of the Americas
New York, New York 10020

First Fireside Edition 1993
Published in 1987 by Prentice Hall Press
A Division of Simon & Schuster Inc.
Originally published by Don Fleming Seminars Publishing Co.

FIRESIDE and colophon are registered trademarks of
Simon & Schuster Inc.
Text design by C. Linda Dingler
Cover design and illustrations by Bill Melendez

Manufactured in the United States of America

20 19 18 17 16 15 14 13 12

Library of Congress Cataloging-in-Publication Data

Fleming, Don.
How to stop the battle with your child.

Bibliography: p.
Includes index.
1. Child rearing. I. Balahoutis, Linda. II. Title.
HQ769.F538 1987   649'.1   86-17020
ISBN 0-671-76349-0

I dedicate this book to the five most important women in my life: my mother, Genevieve—I'll always remember her caring and loving ways; my wife, Pamela; my sister, Millicent; my niece, Denel; and my newest love, my grandniece, Nicole, who was born April 24, 1986.

Acknowledgments

I want to thank Berea St. John, who encouraged me to become a psychotherapist and who, for many years, gave me the kind of inspiration that enabled me to achieve many of the goals in my life. Second, thanks to Estelle Sudnow, who was my first-year supervisor in graduate training at Florida State University and for whom I have the greatest respect. She gave me excellent supervision for which I will always be grateful. I am particularly indebted to Susan Schuster and Marilyn Lebow, who read the manuscript and contributed suggestions and criticism. Thanks to my sister, Millie Lupiani, who encouraged me and who has been one of my biggest boosters. My love to Denel Duprez, my niece, who is so important to me. My love to Brian Lupiani, my terrific nephew, for his interest in the success of the book. My deepest appreciation to Edward Lupiani, my brother-in-law, director of Elementary Education, Baldwin Park Unified School District, for his professional contribution in assisting with the development of this book.

I would also like to acknowledge Al Cartwright, director of Career Education and Special Projects, and Joe Spirito, director of Instructional Services, Baldwin Park Unified School District, for their concern and interest in the book. I wish to acknowledge Dr. Susan Brown for her inspiration over the years and for her friendship as a colleague. Also, thanks to Dr. Frank Williams for his long-time support as both colleague and friend. A special thanks to my wife, Pamela, for putting up with me during the writing of this book and for being very loving and understanding.

I'd also like to thank all those who through the years have assisted me in my career. And I cannot forget the many parents with whom I have worked, and who helped me develop the kind of experience and knowledge that has made this book possible.

Last, I would like to give a special thanks to my agent, Sherry Robb, who with humor, intelligence, and sincerity helped me get my book published. Thanks must also go to PJ Dempsey, my editor, who is great to work with and really made the process of publishing this book a very enjoyable and positive experience.

Contents

Introduction

What—another book on parenting? You might be thinking, "Aren't there enough of those? Haven't we read everything there is to read about it already?" Yes, there have been many books on parenting. Most give excellent suggestions. Some work at least part of the time.

However, if you are reading this book, I assume that nothing is working. By this time you have armed yourself with countless helpful hints from different sources. Then your child confronts you with a variation of the standard crisis, leaving you thinking, "Now what? This is different from situation No. 46!" After all your preparation, *your kid is still winning*! This may lead you to believe that he, too, is boning up on the subject of parenting. Maybe he is even attending seminars on "How to Make Life More Difficult for Your Parents."

This is a book for the average parent, whether single or with an intact family. It is for you if you have become locked into a chronic, unending battle with your child over specific attitudes or behavior patterns in daily routines such as going to the market, going to bed, or picking up toys. It presents step-by-step methods of unlocking the struggle. Children's deep psychological problems are not dealt with in this book. Instead, practical suggestions are offered about everyday dilemmas that parents have difficulty controlling. Also, this book will be of benefit to teachers and other professionals who work with parents.

Experiencing frustration more than once may have given you a strong desire to run away from home. But you are not crazy or a bad parent! Ambivalence, anger, and frustration are all understand-able results of this continuous locked-in struggle with your child.

You may still ask how this book is different from other parenting books. Let's look at four basic categories with differing approaches to child-rearing and examine their values and drawbacks.

The Developmental Approach. Developmental psychology tells us what to expect from children at various stages of development. Books based on this approach are very informative about every aspect of normal child development, such as what age your child should start toileting and when he should stop sucking his thumb. They do not help you deal with the child who picks a fight with his brother every time you take him somewhere in the car. If you are locked into a struggle with your five-year-old, you do not want to know how bad (or good) he'll be when he is eight years old.

The Behaviorial Approach. This approach stresses changing behavior through the use of a punishment and reward system. This technique has value and may at first glance seem similar to the approach presented in this book. The drawback to the behaviorist approach is that the parent relies too heavily on punishment and reward, and fails to incorporate feelings. Also, the parent does not see how his own behavior impacts on the child. In the behaviorial approach, the system can become more important than the rela-tionship.

The Firm Discipline Approach. Currently there are a number of popular books that suggest very firm discipline. In part this is a reaction to the very permissive approach. The point of this ap-proach is that parents are really in charge, and the only way to make this clear to kids is with strong discipline. However, this method does not allow parents the flexibility to be firm and at the same time tender and sensitive. Secondly, and most important, this approach ignores the impact of the parent's behavior on the child. It fails to make parents take a hard look at their behavior patterns, which might prolong the problem even when there is strong discipline.

The Permissive Approach. In the permissive approach, the child's feelings are foremost in importance. Parents are taught to share their feelings with their child and to be sensitive to her feelings. Now then, feelings are truly important *in their place*. However, some books advocating the permissive method give the impression that all you have to do as a parent is to be sensitive and reflect feelings. Then, as if by magic, your child will never again tear around the house like a banshee. Overreflection of feelings gives a child too much power and control. That approach fails to acknowledge either the human limitation of the child—or the job of the parent. A child must learn that there are times she needs to limit her feelings and regain control of herself.

THE JOB OF PARENTING

Parenting is the hardest job in the world. Most parents adequately grasp the features of the job that include taking care of their child's basic needs, helping to structure daily routines, showing their child love, providing experiences that give the child both pleasure and learning, and teaching life's values. Most parents make every effort to do these things with caring and involvement. However, many parents do not understand how to prepare their child for life by teaching him appropriate behavior. This means not only understanding your child's behavior and feelings, but also using appropriate consequences when his behavior is not acceptable. Remember, too, you cannot teach your child anything if you do not notice how your own behavior affects him. This does not mean you have to feel guilty or self-conscious, just become more aware.

If you want to change your child's behavior, the desired change must have priority. Teaching him to be an effective human being is sometimes more important than cleaning the kitchen, going shopping, or keeping up with the Joneses. Your priority, if you want to change his behavior, is to focus on the interaction.

From my seminars and family treatment work over the years, I have seen that parents can be taught to see how they get locked into negative situations and how to unlock these situations. This book will help you learn how to unlock behavior that interferes with effective discipline. You will begin to understand the differences in your agenda and your child's agenda: for example, your goal when going out to a restaurant is to relax, but your child sees it as an irresistible opportunity to explore new and exciting territory.

Tedious and frustrating daily situations will be covered as well. You will learn how to turn a negative situation with your child into a positive one. By being aware of and controlling your behavior, you will learn to deal with these difficulties. The chapter on discipline will give you concepts that are practical and workable.

I am also offering a serious but lighthearted perspective that will improve the quality of the relationship with your child. Many aspects of our modern life-styles make parenting more difficult today. The rising divorce rate and the changing roles of males and females are among the factors that seem to be working against tranquil parent/child relationships. These situations can be handled in appropriate, resourceful ways.

The extensive work I've done with parents has given me a deep respect for the difficulties of their job. Many parents who are extremely effective still get locked into struggles with their children, and they find the experience exasperating. It is with great empathy for parents that I write this book. I hope my approach and examples will ultimately relieve the burden that parents feel when trapped into battles with their children.

HOW TO USE THIS BOOK AND HOW NOT TO

Even though the approach is "step-by-step," this is not a prescription or recipe book. This is a book designed to give parents a concrete way to focus on specific types of problems. The sequence of "steps," the consequences, and the dialogue are adaptable to your own needs. Sometimes the consequences I suggest may not fit your situation or feel right to you. Still, I hope that when you are locked in, they will help you to think about different ways of looking at your situation with your child, and what you might do about it. In this book, some ways of talking to children may seem repetitious, but that is because you need to learn that many circumstances, though different, having similar approaches. Also, this book does not have right and wrong answers, so do not take it to your spouse and say, "See, I told you so." Both of you should use it flexibly.

If a child is ill or under unusual stress, consequences that would normally be effective will sometimes cause regression in his behavior. Under these circumstances, feel free to limit the use of consequences until the stress has been considerably reduced. This is the time to be very understanding about your child's feelings.

PART I
DISCIPLINE

1

Looking at Ineffective Discipline

Through the ages, parents have indeed learned some ingenious techniques to discipline children. Screaming at the top of your lungs is an old favorite, employed to get your kid to listen. At the very least, you can increase your lung power! Now if this fails altogether, you really have a bonus: you have lost your voice and you won't have to talk for a year. When your lungs give out and you realize that the yelling hasn't worked, you usually threaten the child with statements such as, "If you don't stop that, you are really going to get it!" Generally, this is ineffective since you and your child have not figured out what "it" is.

The next remark is a real signal that you're irritated—"I'm at the end of my rope!" If that doesn't work, and it doesn't, you turn to other techniques out of sheer desperation. They are age-old, despite their ineffectiveness.

The Cold Shoulder. You stay angry at your child all day, using clever, hurt looks that you know your child notices. Designed to make him feel guilty or upset, this technique usually clarifies nothing. It is a good way to keep him anxious, though. A variation of this is the famous, "I am *not* hurt" look, which consists of not looking at your child for hours and answering in cold, distant tones.

The "How Dare You Talk to Me like That?" Maneuver. This involves a raised eyebrow—usually the right—and a curled lip. This is something you might have to practice in the mirror, but when you have perfected it, your child will tend to take you *very* seriously—even though it's quite ineffective in changing the child's behavior.

The Storm Trooper Attack. This may well rank among the most notorious of tactics. You wait until you're totally enraged—having asked your kid twenty times to stop what he's doing—and then you finally go berserk. The strategy consists of jumping out of your chair with your arms straight out, ready to choke anyone in your path, and running at the child with all the force of a hurricane (don't forget to bulge your eyes out of their sockets). It's amazing how quickly your child will move when you do this. He finally believes that you mean business. One danger in doing this, though, is that if your friends catch you, you will probably be termed crazy.

The Blue-in-the-face Approach. This is otherwise known as the "Please help me, I'm drowning" routine. When your child does something over and over, you respond by saying, "OK, OK, if you must do it, go ahead! Just leave me alone for a few minutes!" What he learns is that, "If I bug Mom and Dad enough, they will give in!" or "I must really be a pain in the neck!" Again, this approach doesn't accomplish anything, and you will end up with terminal frustration.

The Tune-out Trick. Many times fathers seem to be guiltier in this area than mothers. The scene occurs when your child is running around the house wielding a butcher knife, pursued by his mother in her best Storm Trooper fashion, and father, with a newspaper up to his face, calmly says, "Cut out all that noise," tuning out the fact that he has anything to do with what's going on . . . or that he should have anything to do with it. In the meantime, mother starts prophesying that her child will turn into a juvenile delinquent, or she will call a close friend and complain that her husband is a bad father. However, with effective tuning out, fathers won't even hear the defamatory remarks.

Back-of-the-hand Approach. Spanking has been around since the beginning of time, and some parents might insist that this is a technique that works. I'm not going to insist that it doesn't work, some of the time. Hearing parents repeatedly talk about this issue, I've learned that it does nothing but create more frustration for them as well as their children. As we discussed, yelling increases your lung power, or it might scare the heck out of your kid, but it generally has no effect at all. Similarly, spanking certainly gets your child's attention and temporarily makes an impact. But as a main source of discipline, I've rarely seen it work. Out of fear, a child may respond, but the child grows up resentful of a parent's power. He internalizes a great deal of anger. This will be taken out somewhere, frequently on his kids—who will then vent anger on their kids, and so forth. Generally, we spank for two reasons: to change the child's behavior and/or to release frustration. An occasional spank on the rear end doesn't do any damage to a child. Occasionally, it gets the point across quite quickly. But as a primary way of trying to control a child's behavior, or to teach him a "lesson," it's never worked and it never will. Power and anger don't make us want to improve.

This section was not designed to make you feel stupid or ill-suited for parenting (even though you may be saying, "It's too late for that!"). My intention is to illustrate those behavior patterns parents are most likely to get locked into. Until you are aware of what you are doing, there is no way to effectively change your child's behavior. In order to assess how you are *really* communicating, you must be aware of what you verbalize and how it sounds. Additionally, you must evaluate your nonverbal communications (such as the preceding examples). You can probably name five thousand things your kid does that you don't like. When you're asked what you do, however, rarely will you say anything other than: "Well, I hadn't thought about that." Many children in therapy tell me they don't listen because they know you probably won't follow through on what you say. This means they are very good observers of your behavior!

To bring into focus the impact that your behavior has on your child's behavior, the next section will take a closer look at the storm trooper and blue-in-the-face types and give insight into unlocking these patterns.

WHY PARENTS DISCIPLINE

Now that we have looked at some types of ineffective discipline, you're probably wondering what does work. To understand, we must first look at why you discipline your child and how you choose your style of discipline. Anger and frustration at your child's behavior is one reason; teaching your child to mind is another. Additionally, you may discipline from the modeling you received from your own parents. It may be the only method you know. If your father spanked you each time you got out of line, it is likely that you follow this method with your own child. Some parents overreact to the method they were raised with and use tactics that are just the opposite of the ones their parents used.

You might already be saying, "What's this guy talking about? When my kid starts throwing ice-cream sandwiches around, I just want him to stop." This might be the time when you resort to disciplining out of anger or frustration.

Your child's failure to react to your brand of discipline carries with it a complexity of concerns. You probably have expectations of achievement and success for him. His refusal to respond to discipline frightens you. You imagine his whole future to be in jeopardy. Of course, this isn't true. You will see that coping with complex situations has to do with understanding the differences between your and your child's agendas, observing your own behavior and its impact, and using appropriate consequences. All this can be done while remaining sensitive to your child's feelings.

MAKING A NEGATIVE SITUATION POSITIVE

Discipline is difficult if it results in negative feelings toward your child. It makes you and your child feel bad. You do not want these feelings to linger. You want to leave him with a clear understanding of what is required of him. You do not want to leave him feeling confused or guilty. He is not a terrible person because he behaves in a way you don't like.

Most parents think they are being clear when they are not. They overreact to inappropriate behavior and hardly react at all to improvements. You can make the whole issue of discipline easier by emphasizing even the smallest improvements.

For example, Mother says, "I have tried to tell you that it helps me when you don't leave your toys around the house. I have so much to do. Dad's coming home, and I have to feed the baby. If you could only learn to do this."

The child says, "Yes, Mom. I'm sorry. I didn't mean to. I'll never do it again."

Mom: "Good, that helps me a lot."

Johnny then runs into the bedroom, starts picking up his toys, and becomes distracted with one toy.

Mother comes in and says, "I thought you promised that you'd never do it again." She again lectures on how the child is responsible for her misery.

Here is a more effective style of communication. In essence, we will emphasize Johnny's beginning effort and help him to refocus on the appropriate behavior. Once she sees that Johnny is distracted, Mom says, "I can see that you got a good start. Let's get it finished so you will have time to do other things. I really like your effort." The child understands that he's made a mistake, yet he feels appreciated for his good intentions.

Another way to make a negative situation positive is to talk to your child about his behavior at times when you are not under stress. For example, if you've struggled with him about eating breakfast, you might wait until he comes home from school. You might say, "I know we had a difficult time this morning. I will try to let you know what I want without getting angry. I hope you will learn to listen better."

Children frequently listen better when the storm has passed. This means you must remember to come back to the disputed issue. You might be tempted to forget all about it because you are concerned about upsetting your child. If you do this, you will miss a great learning opportunity. These quiet talks give you a chance to clarify issues, share feelings, and reinforce the notion that problems can be solved.

When you have been locked into a struggle, it is understandable that you are anxious to change not only the *behavior* of your child but his *negative attitude* as well. You may be operating at such a high level of frustration that if he does not respond immediately to your request, you become irritated and frustrated; possibly you are so affected by your child's contentiousness that you feel enough rage to reject him. These are very common feelings. But you must be realistic about attitude change. It comes slowly—not just for children but also for adults!

In order to take a negative situation and make it positive, you must focus on the *change*, however slight, in your child's *behavior* rather than the snotty look on his face.

For example, if you tell your child, "I want you to go to your room and clean up now," and he doesn't move as quickly as you'd like, don't use the "out-of-socket" yank to pull him to his room. Do not say things such as, "Take that ugly smirk off your face this minute!" Focus only on the positive change in your child's behavior.

Ideally, you should say nothing about the look or attitude of your child. Simply state: "I know it's hard for you to clean up your room, but I'm glad you're able to listen to me." This gives him the feeling that the effort, not his inappropriate response, is what is important. Once you gain better control, you can begin to work on your child's *attitude*.

UNDERSTANDING THE ADULT'S AGENDA AND THE CHILD'S AGENDA

In order to understand how to discipline and how to change negative behavior into positive behavior, you must first have a better understanding of the adult's agenda and the child's agenda. These agendas include the values, expectations, and aims of the parent/child relationship. And you expect your ideal program to work even though there is a difference in the way your child views the identical situation. When you understand the difference, you will begin to see the origin of conflict. Constant quarreling between the parent and a seemingly difficult child may be due to a simple misunderstanding between agendas.

For example, you are standing in a movie line with your three-year-old, and your agenda is for your child to be quiet and cooperative. Yet you are restless, shifting from one foot to the other, griping to the theater manager, "This darn movie should have started fifteen minutes ago!"

Your child's agenda is to take this boring situation and make it as interesting as possible. This might entail breaking loose from your hand, making faces, or picking fights with the kids next in line. Your child, in a sense, is doing what he should be doing. He is trying to make a dull situation interesting—with a method you consider inappropriate.

To the young child, the world is a wondrous place. He is continually discovering something new. His primary goal is to continue discovery, and to experience the world on his own terms. To accomplish his agenda he must get around you, "those people," his parents, whose agenda seems opposed to his. In other words, a large part of your agenda is to interfere with your child's attempts at exploration and to teach him appropriate behavior. Once you understand this, you will not take his defiance, his seeming indifference to your unhappiness, so personally. The next time he disappears under the table in a restaurant, you might even find it humorous to know that, in a way, he's doing what he's supposed to be doing.

In other words, a certain amount of conflict between you and your child is normal and necessary. After all, your child's agenda is to test you and the world.

Your agenda, whether conscious or unconscious, is to raise your child with behavior that meets your standards, especially your standards for social appropriateness. You want a well-behaved youngster who never shows disrespect, and who (miraculously) understands your needs, regardless of the way you communicate those needs. You want these qualities to appear with as little struggle as possible.

It is much easier to understand the idea of agendas theoretically than when under the stress of the moment. When your child is darting in and out of department store aisles, it's hard to remember that he's only testing limits.

Simply put, agendas define tasks. A child's job is to test many things in his world; a parent's job is to set limits to these tests. For example, your four-year-old is climbing on the kitchen counter, exploring new territory. You say, "Don't climb on that counter! You'll fall and get hurt!"

But your child, undaunted, pays no attention. Your agenda is to teach him about danger as well as the necessity of following parental rules. Your child's agenda, if he could verbalize it, would be "I have to find this out for myself! It's fun to climb, and who asked for your opinion, anyway?"

Children over the age of six have their own agendas as well as clear ideas of what they want. Instead of whining, throwing tantrums, and fussing at you, a child this age will attempt a long dialogue to convince you to see things his way. Sometimes parents are so impressed with the child's verbal ability that they become confused and give in, or don't know what to say. Or they may say to themselves, "I'm going to tape this kid's mouth shut if he says one more word! I get the heebie-jeebies every time I think about telling him something, because I know he's going to try to argue me out of it!"

This technique of lengthy conversation is the child's way of experimenting with how the world works. Children have strong feelings about what they want, and their agenda may be to try to argue you out of your point of view. They have discovered that many times it works!

In other words, your child is not being defiant just to taunt you. By understanding crucial differences in agendas, observing your own behavior, and then using appropriate consequences, you will learn to unlock the ongoing struggle between you and your child.

OBSERVING PARENTAL BEHAVIOR

Observing your own behavior does not mean standing and looking at yourself in the mirror all day; that's called narcissism. And it isn't the same as knowing yourself by having your astrological chart done. It simply means being as *clear or clearer about your reaction to your child as you are about his reaction to you*. It means being very conscious of the differences in your moods and how this affects his behavior. It means taking an extra moment to think of what you want from your child. Unless you are fully aware of your own parental style, you won't be aware of why the relationship isn't working.

Parents often don't realize how strong an impact they have on their children. This is particularly true when parents are ineffective in trying to get their child to respond as expected to parental directions or requests. It is very common for parents to be unaware of their conduct toward their child. When you're locked into a struggle with your child, the intensity of your frustration is clearly felt and resistance to you will increase.

In order to learn to become a better observer of your own behavior, think about this issue from an adult perspective. Suppose you haven't done something your spouse has asked you to do.

He approaches you like this: "Dammit, how many times do I have to ask you to pick up my shirts? You're driving me crazy!"

Your likely response, verbalized or not, is probably, "Why don't you sit on it? Stop telling me what to do!"

The person who initiates such an interaction (in this case, your spouse) is usually unaware of how much impact he has and how his approach creates resistance in the other person. Since this isn't a marital book, let's get back to the child. If you approach your child in the manner described above, it is likely that he won't tell you or even clearly understand what his feelings are, but you can bet his reaction won't be much different from what your own would be!

Children feel your attitude toward them, but they don't always understand it. For example, a mother or father may say to young children, "If you kids don't stop fighting, I'm going to get rid of both of you." One child shows no obvious response, and the other child cries. The second child has taken your threat very seriously and wonders if you mean it. The first child is probably startled by your comment but feels secure enough with you to know that you sometimes talk like that when you're upset.

What both children hear is your attitude. Your instruction to stop fighting is obscured by your negative tone.

A parent who's become a good observer might say, "If both of you kids don't control yourselves and stop fighting right now, you can't play together the rest of the evening." (Most kids, even if they're killing one another, want some time together.) If children don't get along, an aware parent will choose a consequence such as sending the children to different rooms. This doesn't mean that your expectation (that they get along) will always be realized, but it is an example of the way a parent can be clear and focused.

Children give many signals that they are impacted by parents. These signals are often not understood. For example, you say in anger, "Sometimes you kids make me wish I never had children!" The children go on with their play or walk away. Two weeks later, when you're feeling fine, your child walks up to you.

"Mom, I hate you 'cause you said you don't want me!"

You're astonished, and reply, "I didn't say that!"

"Yes, you did! You said you wish you never had kids!" your child replies.

Observing your behavior means really listening to your communication and realizing that no matter how a child responds, he feels and is affected by what you say.

Questions a good observer must ask would be: "How often do I praise instead of criticize? How often do I take for granted what my child does well without commenting on it? How often do I ask my child to do something? Two times? Four times?" If you have to ask more than twice without taking some action, you're teaching your child that he has the right to delay what you expect of him. In this case, you should be aware that you are as much a part of the problem as he is.

In summary, we all like the feeling of being talked to in a supportive way. Understandably, it isn't possible for parents to be aware of their behavior at all times, especially when they're struggling with a child; but if parents want to unlock the struggle with their children, they must become more aware of the importance of their own behavior.

Below are some parenting styles that will help you define your own approach. I have basically dealt with negative methods, in order to help you become more reflective—not to point out your deficiency as a parent.

The Overtalker

This parent verbalizes into the sunset. You explain, reexplain, comment, point out . . . until you get to the point where you haven't noticed that your child has walked out and is in the den watching television. You become so immersed in your own verbalizations that you don't know when your child is no longer listening. You miss all his clues—yawning, making noises, running away. When you overtalk, you are so involved in what you are saying that it's impossible to observe your own behavior. Parents influenced by the permissive or reflective approaches frequently become overtalkers and overlisteners.

The Overlistener

You are the parent who listens to the child's every feeling as if it were a Shakespearean drama. Your child says, "Suzy hurt my feelings." You tune in with such dramatic effect that sometimes your child starts out only mildly upset but ends up feeling that something horrible must have happened because you are so concerned. The overlistener has an antenna that picks up sounds—particularly crying and screaming—from two blocks to two miles away. You not only listen but tune into things that are sometimes none of your business.

You may hear your child talking to a friend about a mean kid at school when, all of a sudden, you break down the door and announce, "If you're upset, you can always talk to me."

Your kid looks up with bug eyes and thinks, "How did she know we were even talking about that other kid?" Then he wonders how the issue became so serious when he was just "rapping" with a friend.

Your child learns that he may never stand on his own two feet because you're always there for him every moment of the day. This inappropriate emotional response is a marvelous way for your child to get attention for situations that he should handle on his own. In other words, your child can become too emotionally needy if you are an overlistener.

The Undertalker

"Uh huh." "No." "Yes." "Don't bother me now, I'm busy!" "Go talk to your mother/father." These are the phrases your child hears if you are an undertalker. Most of the monosyllabic responses are accompanied by a blank stare. Sometimes a parent falls into this category without really being an undertalker. But it is important to note the effect on your child if this is your regular style. Your child might only approach you now in a negative manner. For example, the child may always act frustrated with you because he never senses your interest. Children sense when their words and feelings seem to be unimportant to adults.

The Complainer

If you are a complainer, you are always telling your child everything that's wrong. "Your room is a mess!" "Look at your hair—it
looks like a rat's nest!" "Things would be a lot better around here
if you'd just listen to me for once!" Or "I could have done so
many things with my life if you had been more cooperative." Com-
plainers are different from overtalkers because they belittle and
blame their children and everyone but themselves. They are the
ultimate poor observers of their own behavior and the impact it
has on their children. A complainer's child may grow to believe
that his parents find him unworthy, which will make him feel very
angry or hurt.

The Helpless Parent

The parent who throws up his hands in the air conveys to his child,
"I can't do anything with you." The child develops the sense that
he's the parent. The helpless parent gives in often and uses bribes.
When your child is at the market screaming wildly that he won't
leave until he gets five Hershey bars and a Pepsi, you, the helpless
parent, look to see if anyone is watching, and then stuff the five
Hershey bars and Pepsi in the basket. Typical comments of the
helpless parent are, "I just don't know what to do with this child.
He won't listen to a thing I say." "Go ahead and do it. You're going
to do what you want anyway." Parental helplessness teaches a
child that being a tyrant works: if he's dramatic enough or puts up
strong resistance, good ole Mommy or Daddy will give in. This
child never learns the limits of anything.

The Reactor

As a reactor, you are not known for having a slow fuse. You yell
and holler as fast as the overtalker talks. You are probably angry,
upset, or frustrated 80 percent of the day. You are so ready to
react that your child becomes gun-shy and puts his hands on his
ears in anticipation of your next banshee scream. Sometimes
neighbors take bets on the mood of the reactor in the morning

and what time the first incident will take place. If this description is making you feel guilty, that is not my intent. I'm just pointing out the impact of your behavior.

Children have a variety of reactions to this style of parenting. One is to avoid the parents and not to get close to them. Sometimes the child picks up the same pattern of behavior. Reactor parents will say, "I can't figure it out—my child reacts to every little thing!" This is another example of not being a good observer.

Your child will never learn to trust your feelings when you react to everything. It is scary and confusing. Sometimes parents whose style is that of a reactor will ask me why their child will not talk to them! Being poor observers, they don't see how difficult it is to communicate with a person whose reactions can never be predicted.

The Diverter

This parent avoids conflict and will not set limits on a child's behavior. Total avoidance of confrontation is the diverter's tactic. A diverter technique for getting a child into bed is, "Oh, Honey, come into your bedroom. I brought you something new and I want to show it to you." Before the child has a chance to blink, his clothes are pulled off with one hand; his pajamas are put on with the other. When the kid realizes he's been tricked, he might have a tantrum. Then you have to soothe him with statements like, "I didn't mean to upset you." This is fundamentally dishonest. When your child falls down and cries, "It hurts," and he has been badly frightened by the experience, you contradict his pain by saying, "No, it doesn't really hurt . . . oh, look at the pretty little doggie across the street . . . isn't he a pretty doggie? Let's go over and pet him." Your child is merely responding to his feelings, but as a diverter, you don't deal with the problem. The diverter's children never know how to handle uncomfortable feelings and never learn that it is OK, and even necessary, to occasionally struggle with uncomfortable situations.

The Threatener

This style depends on empty threats and no follow-through. "I want you inside this house this minute . . . or else!" Or, "If you don't turn off that darn TV right now, you're going to get it!" Or, "How many times do I have to tell you you're not going out to play unless you clean up that messy room?" The threatener thinks there is magic in the power of the threat. The empty threat conveys, "I say a lot but I don't do too much about it." The child learns that his parents are often unhappy with him. He responds to the negative attitude with hurt or anger—and defiance. But that's not what parents want!

The preceding examples don't fit everyone totally, but it is important to think about them and become aware of how unclear your communication can be with your child. As a good observer-parent, you should be keenly aware of how your style and moods affect his behavior. This means taking an extra moment to think of what you want from your child. Unless you are fully aware of your *exact* request and *how* you request it, there isn't much hope that his behavior will change.

How many times has your child said to you, "Can I have a snack?" You say, "Sure." Then you walk into the kitchen and see that he has taken enough ingredients for ten sandwiches out of the refrigerator, with two of them in his mouth and the rest on the counter in front of him. When you ask him, "What in the heck is going on?" he responds by saying triumphantly, "But you said I could have a snack!" Your typical reply is, "I didn't mean *that* kind of snack!"

Being clear means to remember to observe your reaction. You responded to what your child asked. He wanted a snack, and you did not qualify any limitations. Now you're probably thinking, "I can understand that from a child who is four or five, but my nine-year-old should know better." Many nine-year-olds (even if they know better) are more concerned with their needs than deciphering your words.

To be a better observer, you must be very specific about what you want from your child. You might wonder whether or not you have to walk around second-guessing everything and to always be asking yourself what you want from your child. As you continue reading this book, you will learn that these new observations and concepts need not feel so overwhelming or difficult.

2

Unlocking the Struggle between Parents and Children

When you have been locked in a struggle with your child, you won't significantly alter her behavior until you grasp certain concepts, that is to say, the differences between parents, and the differences between adult and child agendas. You must also remember the importance of using consequences in a step-by-step manner. It is understandable that many parents would prefer not to start with consequences. They want to try something positive first. I certainly agree that it would be preferable, but many children need firm limits and will only respond when you show them you are the one really in control.

There are some positive steps, such as praise and encouragement, that can unlock many situations with a seemingly unresponsive child. If you've already tried these techniques without results, the locked-in behavior patterns that exist between you call for a need to look at the way you use consequences. This section will conceptualize how to do this in a constructive, caring way that will change a child's behavior.

First Step

Give praise for any positive act by the child. For example, instead of saying, "Why does it take you so long to do this?" try, "Even though it took you a little while to do it, I can see you are really picking up your toys nicely." Another encouraging example is, "I know you don't like to pick up toys, but let's do it now, and then you'll have more time to play."

All parents give encouragement now and then, but parents who are not aware of their own behavior do things inconsistently and without self-critical insight.

Instead of this negative response: "If I have to tell you one more time to clean your room, I'm going to lock it and you'll never get in it again!" a parent can substitute a positive response, saying, "If you clean your room now, we can play a game after dinner." This is a reward for paying attention to a request. Another example would be: "After you get to bed on time, I'll read you a story. This will teach you that it's not so difficult for you to learn to follow rules about bedtime."

Second Step

A way of encouraging specific guidelines for your child is to make a daily chart. This chart can have three to six listings of activities for which she is rewarded for completing *any* task; there are no losses for her. One of the activities on the chart should be very easy to do. Each time she completes one of the tasks, she gets a star on the chart. At the end of the day, if she receives three stars, she will get a reward. The rewards can come from a grab bag of little candies, chewing gum, and toys from a penny-candy machine. Your child can get more than one reward, depending on how you decide to work the chart system. This will help her pay attention to rewards. It is all right for a young child to be unaffected by adult tasks and standards of order.

Along with rewards, parents should convey praise to the child verbally. "Boy, you got two stars today, and that's a real good start. I'm very proud of you! And if you keep doing this well, it probably won't be hard for you to get more."

If your child has a bad day, say, "I know you didn't get any stars today, and you must feel bad. But remember, you can start over again tomorrow. Then you can get some of the things you like."

In the two preceding steps, I have shown examples of how to use praise and encouragement to help you get your child to respond without the use of consequences. To be realistic, for some children, you may need to use the positive aspects that I've discussed, in

	Sun	Mon	Tues	Wed	Thurs	Fri	Sat
Listens to Rules							
Cleans Room							
Sets Table							

addition to consequences. Now I'm going to talk about steps in a structure that can teach you to use consequences in a simple and clear manner.

First Step

I realize it is very difficult not to say something harsh when you've had a pattern of frustration and your child is not obeying. But learning to be a good observer means having more control than your child does. You cannot expect her to respond favorably if you truly don't understand how important this concept is.

Remember to be aware of *how* you request things of your child. Be conscious of your attitude and tone of voice. Think of how you like to be talked to and how you react when someone talks to you in an irrational manner. When you are upset, your child focuses on your frustration and anger instead of your instruction to her. That is not the focal point you want. After a contentious situation, ask yourself how you handled the problem instead of analyzing how your child handled it! This will help you become aware of what you were doing. Once you compare the difference between your old style and your new one, you will see the impact your attitude has on your child's behavior. Recognizing that your attitude is a major cause of your child's reactions is the first step in changing her behavior.

If you are very busy or in a bad mood or just plain tired, you would probably have difficulty controlling a child's behavior. Try not to say anything when you feel overwhelmed; you will only respond ineffectively.

Second Step

Here you are learning to talk to your child about the new process of consequences. As you begin to institute new approaches, you will need to help her understand these changes.

When starting off, don't wait until the first incident to reveal your major war plan. This is one of those rare times when you let your "enemy" know why you are changing strategy, because your "enemy" is the child you care deeply about. You are not out to win the battle in order to defeat her, but to make both of you feel better.

You would start out by telling your child, "When you don't listen or follow our rules, Mommy and/or Daddy yell too much. We are going to try some new rules. Some of them may seem very hard. Since we feel it is so very important, you need to learn to do what we tell you."

Then you could give your child one good example of the problem, such as, "You usually don't pick up your toys when I ask you to, even though I have screamed at you nine times already. This isn't going to happen anymore. From now on if you have a hard time listening to me I will tell you twice to pick up your toys. If you don't listen, you will have to go to bed earlier. I hope you will listen, so that I don't have to put you to bed early."

This kind of dialogue is generalized and can be adapted for other situations. Again, this is not done during the heat of battle. You have already sat down with your child and told her about the new rules.

Third Step

The aim here is to be consistent. This does not mean doing something 100 percent of the time. It means that when you do something, do it the same way all the time—if it has worked. Therefore, a parent who is having trouble following through would do better to follow through 50 percent of the time. Try not to say anything if you feel weak about follow-through, because it only increases the problem; being a good observer means being aware of this weakness. When you feel irritable or out of sorts, it's better to let things go by. Otherwise, when you ask your child to do something and she doesn't do it immediately, chances are you will become the reactor or the storm trooper. Then your child will resent you even more.

It's better to say something like this: "Mom is very tired today, so if you don't want to take your bath, I'll let it go. But it doesn't change the rules for tomorrow." I'd much rather see a child a little dirty and have good feelings continue between parent and child.

Obviously, if you are always in a bad mood, none of this advice will work. But if this is the way you feel some of the time, it doesn't mean you are being inconsistent. Consistency means not allowing yourself to become diverted from disciplining your child. It always means verbalizations followed by actions. And never ask for something more than twice. If you find yourself asking your child to clean her room ten times, you should ask yourself why.

Fourth Step

You must make your request in specific terms. Don't say, "Clean up that mess!" "Get off that telephone," and, "When are you going to clean up your room?" Those are common, nonspecific requests that mean nothing more to kids than parents babbling into the sunset.

Instead, your request should be in this form: "Jane, I want your room cleaned up before dinner." "I will give you one more minute on the phone, and then I'm coming in to see that you hang it up." "I want your toys picked up before you go out to play."

Fifth Step

This is where to use appropriate consequences for your child. Instead of reacting out of anger, frustration, or helplessness, ask yourself what things are important to her. Consequences should deprive a child of pleasure.

Children from three to six years old usually respond to consequences such as: (1) sitting in a chair for a brief time with nothing to do; (2) being sent to their room; (3) early bedtime; (4) limited outside playtime; (5) no bedtime story. You can think of other consequences for a young child.

Children six through nine will respond to: (1) not being allowed to stay overnight at a friend's house; (2) not being allowed to go to special places; (3) not being allowed to participate.

Sitting in a chair for five minutes is an example of doing nothing. This consequence affects the child because her world is play. Sitting, doing nothing, is boring. This is one time that, as a result of her inappropriate behavior, it is appropriate for her to face boredom.

How you *use* consequences depends on the individual child. Some children will respond to the same consequence over and over. Others will respond to one consequence for only a brief period of time before the impact wanes. In this case, increase the length of the consequence. For example, your child could be sent to her room for only ten minutes and it might not bother her. She might come out and repeat the action that sent her there in the first place. If you are observant, you will see that sending her to her room means nothing in itself; the length of time is important. The next time she disobeys, increase the time systematically: first twenty minutes, then thirty. At some point your child will take you seriously, because the time becomes more important than the wish to continue being disobedient. However, you might find that increasing the time doesn't work for the simple reason that your child does not find this boring. She diverts herself and occupies the time by playing games, watching television, or listening to the radio. Therefore, you must remove these items from the room so she will face the full significance of boredom.

Remember, your child's initial agenda is to ignore you. She will continue her actions and hope that you will give up, as usual. But as you increase the consequences, she will then know that you mean business. A child hates to lose playtime, or to be sent to her room to sit in a chair. This is like doing nothing at all.

You might now be saying to yourself, "But I've tried all this stuff!" But have you tried it *systematically*, over and over, for a two-week period? This leads to the next stage.

Sixth Step

You learn to be aware of how quickly you are ready to give up if one step doesn't work. Your reaction might be, "What's the use? Nothing works!" When you have been locked into a struggle for any length of time, you must realize that sometimes *your child's behavior is likely to get worse before it gets better*. It's a good sign if it gets worse; then you know you're making an impact.

Basically, your child is thinking, "I don't believe what these people are doing. They're acting different, and it's making me uncomfortable. But if I hold out long enough, they'll give up like they always do!" She is usually right. It is common for parents to give up quickly rather than sticking to a new technique. You may have been so exasperated for so long that your level of frustration is extremely high. If you are this type of parent, you will react by quitting the first time your child indicates the new technique has no effect on her behavior. But she is not going to instantly show you the impact you're having on her when you have been locked in a struggle for a long time. You can't expect her to say right away, "Gee, making me change is really a great idea. It's much better than yelling and screaming like before!"

You must realize that your child's attitude is not going to change immediately. If you expect her to show you that she approves of your new rules, you are not being observant. This will be a drastic change from the struggle you've been locked into. If nothing else, it will take time for you to reflect on the differences in your interactions with your child. Remember how many times you couldn't easily and lovingly make changes in your own behavior when your spouse or friend asked you to. Children have the same feelings, and they have every right to struggle with their attitudes as you do.

Seventh Step

You learn to readjust when and if the consequences you tried did not work. If your child does not respond when sent to her room or when forced to sit on a chair (even after you increase the time), you must examine the consequences to see what does work and make changes where necessary. You must also do a great job of acting! Pretend that your child's poor behavior is not getting to you, so that she sees you always in control.

When you begin a new technique, it is important to be aware of any change in your child. *Even a little progress is progress.* Because your expectations may be unrealistic, you will be inclined to think that the new techniques don't work. An observant person will notice that the initial change might be mild, but *it is a change.*

For example, if you tell your child to pick up her toys, her reaction might be to shout loudly and say, "No!" stiffening her arms to prove her point. You should firmly let her know what the consequence will be if she doesn't listen to you. If she does pick up her toys, even reluctantly, that is the start of progress. Your child is beginning to give in.

When this happens you should notice a positive change, even a slight one, and reinforce her efforts, just because she tried, by saying, "I know it was hard to listen to me, but I like what you finally did."

This may take a lot of control on your part; I've had parents tell me, "I'd really like to punch my kid in the nose sometimes!" This is, again, an understandable reaction, and it demonstrates the level of frustration that goes along with a locked-in struggle with a child. You are so anxious to have your relationship with your child finally work that you get upset or easily discouraged when things do not change instantly.

I understand this, but effective parenting takes a consistent amount of relearning for the parent. It also takes new ways of looking at your own style and understanding your child in a different way.

When you use these procedures with your child, you are implying that both of you could do better and that you are going to help her. You are also showing her that you are in control of the situation (or can be). Do not infer that she should feel guilty or be blamed for not behaving according to your wishes.

You might think to yourself: "If I'm having a calm day with my child, why should I want to discuss new strategy and potential problem areas?" I understand the concern you may have: such a discussion could bring up bad feelings. However, you are teaching your child and yourself that "loaded" issues can be discussed in a controlled, calm manner. This approach gives her the opportunity to experience change without being overwhelmed or scared.

Stick to one or two issues. Do not try to discuss nineteen things at once. You will only overburden your child, and your conversations will have little meaning. Be observant, and try one specific area at a time. See how that works, and be aware of how effectively or ineffectively you are both handling the situation. If it does not work, go through the steps we have discussed, and try to analyze at what point you did not observe your behavior.

Don't get locked in on consequences. If your child learns to respond well to the new method of discipline, but is having a particularly difficult day, you might want to forego consequences. You could say, "I can see you're really having a difficult time, so I am going to help you clean your room." "I want you to stop whining, and I know you can do it because most of the time you have learned to control yourself so well." These are examples of encouragement and praise that can be used along with or in place of consequences as appropriate.

In later chapters we will discuss specific, day-to-day situations, with examples of how to talk to your child, how to use consequences, and how *not* to talk to your child about locked-in issues. We will redefine problems by understanding the use of agendas, appropriate consequences, and observations of your own behavior.

3

Parental Differences in Discipline

Part of learning to be a good observer is learning to monitor your interaction with your spouse as you both relate to your child. This chapter is about the wide variety of ways that parents interfere with each other's attempts at discipline.

During seminars and therapy, I hear parents' conflicting views about who is the best at raising the kids, who is ruining the kids, who never follows through on discipline, and so forth. Sometimes parents say, "When I am alone with my child, I do just fine!" This sort of declaration betrays your poor cooperation. It also betrays your misunderstanding of the importance of cooperating with your spouse in your child's behalf. When you are alone with your child, he knows he has your attention. You probably make yourself available to him without thinking. As soon as your spouse comes home, you are trying to meet your child's needs and your spouse's needs. Your child wants the attention of both Mommy and Daddy and notices that the attention is split. The only thing for him to do is to act overdemanding, crazy, or wild. Then he can be the center of attention for both parents.

Now is the time to understand why the two of you so often fail to establish a united front. Parental fantasy visualizes "Father Knows Best," (or, since recent role reversals, "Mother Knows Best"). Mother and Father walk into the house, happy children greet them, and everyone gazes adoringly at each other. Then they sit down to a quiet, friendly meal and discuss the plumber who didn't show up and bicycles that need repairs and unfinished homework.

Instead the parent walks in saying under his or her breath, "Can't

I come home to this house once without chaos?" The spouse is saying, "It's more trouble when you are home because the kids get absolutely crazy." Now is the time to understand why the two of you so frequently fail to establish a united front.

The following dialogue exemplifies the lack of communication that often takes place between parents. You can see how this strengthens your child's agenda, which is to establish control by playing one parent against the other.

Father to Mother: "Those kids never listen to you. Can't you get them to shut up for once?" . . . "My mother never had the trouble with her kids that you do!" . . . For the few mothers who don't work: "I don't understand why you can't handle those kids—you don't do anything else all day!" . . . "Just give me a week with those kids and I'll have them in shape!" (also a famous mother-in-law comment) . . . "They're great when you're not here!" And the comment that exasperates wives the most: "Well, they mind when I tell them to do something!"

Mother to Father: "How would you know? You never pay attention to what's going on around here anyway! You're always watching football!" . . . "You're just like my father. He never did anything with the kids!" . . . "If only you could be like Mr. Jones next door. He's so helpful. He even takes care of the kids when Sue goes out." . . . "No wonder the kids don't listen to me. You come in screaming and take over right when I'm beginning to get them settled. Then you take credit for it!"

You can see how warm and loving these comments are! But why do parents indulge in these verbal exchanges? Is it because they should not have married or had children in the first place? Is it because they are vicious, horrible people? I don't think so. In my experience, parents can and will handle these issues when given direction.

Parents fail to agree when dealing with their children for a variety of reasons. Role expectations, stress, and fantasies about what it is like to have children are all part of the story. There are some parents who have a need to use children as scapegoats for their own unresolved problems. For the most part, however, parents have not been well educated about the effects of parental discord on their children. Nor, as far as I know, is there any school for parents that teaches them how to stick together when disciplining their children.

Parental conflicts affect children in different ways. Your child may feel that you don't know what you are doing. He may become confused about which parent he should listen to. He becomes uncertain about the message he receives from one parent when alone versus the message he receives when both parents are together.

For example, a mother says nine times, "If you don't come inside and get to the table right now, you're going to get it." A father jumps in and says to Mother, "What the heck is the matter with you? Can't you make him listen?" The child learns that Dad thinks Mom is inept, inadequate, and incapable.

Body language may also communicate lack of support. Frequently I hear of situations where one parent corrects the child but the other parent picks him up and soothes him shortly after. This type of behavior is a tacit form of criticism and is ultimately not conducive to a child's learning acceptable behavior.

Such seemingly innocent actions keep frustration alive between parents. They broadcast lack of unity to their child. I am sure you've noticed that your child takes advantage of this lack of agreement. He feels that he can get at least one of his parents to take his side. "Daddy, if you are mean to me, I'll just go to Mommy. She'll listen to me," is what he's thinking.

The road out of these parental traps may seem a bit strange at first because it involves a new style of relating.

First Step

Identify the problem areas. Is your child more difficult when both spouses are there? When you are out in public? At mealtime? Both of you should take time to think about how you react when issues arise.

Second Step

Find time to clarify the areas that bother each spouse. Make an effort to phrase your concerns in a nonaccusatory way. A two-year discussion on the subject is not necessary, even though you might feel it will take this long to unravel an ongoing problem. If the purpose of your discussion is to improve your child's reaction as well as yours, then you can speak candidly about how ineffective you both have been.

Third Step

Make firm agreements to support one another. For example, if you are telling your child to go to bed and you are upset because you've already asked him more than twice, your spouse should intervene and say, "I can see you are not listening to Mommy, and she is getting upset. But she is right, so I want you to go to bed." The spouse, in this case, is being supportive rather than critical, and is reinforcing the mutual agreement about disciplining. Your spouse is also letting your child know that he is expected to listen, even though you were too upset. You are being fair to him, while asserting your parental expectations, and you are letting him know that he cannot use one parent to exploit the other's vulnerabilities.

Let's say you have agreed on a bedtime. You come home to find your spouse and child arguing. Your spouse is not following through with your agreement. This is your opportunity to say, "I want Johnny to wait while we go into the other room to discuss this." You have agreed in advance on this procedure. The parent who has lost control goes back and tells the child in a controlled way that he must go to bed. The other parent simply supports that request by saying, "Just listen to your mother/father."

As an alternative technique you might say, "Do you really want Johnny to have more than two chances?" Or, "It looks like you're getting angry because Johnny isn't listening to you." Here you are simply letting your spouse know you're aware of the problem. You don't try to take over or imply that your spouse is a half-wit! You simply cue in the agreed-upon response.

Sometimes you may allow the disciplining parent to proceed without interfering. After the episode is concluded you might say, "Can we talk about what happened with Johnny? It seemed like things didn't work out the way you would have liked."

After this conference, both parents confront their child together, saying, "Look, I'm glad you finally listened. I know I got too mad, and next time I'll try not to do that again. But you must learn to listen better." Your spouse lends support with words like these: "Your daddy is trying to make things better, and I think he's right. You do need to listen. Sometimes, though, we both get too mad." This interchange doesn't entail a five-day seminar—don't be the overtalker. It should not take you longer than one minute.

Going back to your child helps him see that these big, all-powerful people will take responsibility for their role in the encounter. It also teaches him that even when he is wrong, you have the capacity to be very fair. This makes conflict resolution a natural part of your lives, rather than a crisis. Your child may show relief, or he may seem unhappy. Give him time. All of us, adults as well as children, have difficulty letting go of anger or hurt.

If your child is unresponsive, you may say, "I guess you're not ready to hear this, and that's OK. I just want you to know how we feel." You will probably want validation for your improved methods. Remember, he does not know that this change constitutes improvement. It is unfair to ask things of him that take maturity to learn. If you expect your child to hug you and love you for your outpouring of feelings, you are asking for trouble.

Sometimes one parent walks into turmoil without knowing what's going on. Suppose Mother tells Johnny to stay in his room. He sees Daddy strolling by and invites him to play a game. Do not "catch" your spouse and child and ask, "Why are you playing now?" Do not say to your spouse, "You are always interfering when I tell him to do something." Instead, say to your child, "I don't think Daddy knows that I told you to go to your room for not listening to me. I don't think it's time to be playing a game."

For parents with advance agreements, the above statements are heard as cues, not criticism. The appropriate response is, "Your mom is right, I didn't know. We have to stop playing. I know that's hard." Your child receives empathy along with consistent, firm discipline. These techniques are effective whether the parent interferes knowingly or unknowingly.

Sometimes the child will go to one parent without the other parent's knowledge. If he does this habitually, you must follow up each time with, "Have you checked with your mother on this?"

Don't accept his "Yes" at face value. Have your spouse corroborate. Demonstrate that as parents you are together on these issues. If your child says, "You never believe me!" don't say, "You're darn right, kid!" Instead reply, "Sometimes you try to get around us. Until you learn not to, we are going to check with one another."

If your child continues this manipulation by approaching the other parent, you must warn him of a consequence. Don't yell, scream, and say, "Why did you do that?" Let him know that he'll go to bed early or lose playtime—depending on what is important to him. Then add supportively, "I hope you can learn not to go around us. Then you won't have to go to bed early."

Even with these well-thought-out agreements, you may still be so frustrated that you block out rational responses. You might have thought, "This Fleming fellow has got to be crazy to think we can be this reasonable with each other." Some of the dialogue I've suggested may seem artificial, but take a good look (and laugh) at the way you have been dealing with your conflicts. You may find change worth the effort. Most of the couples I work with in my seminars do not find it so difficult to change the structure of their interaction with one another and their children.

Remember, your child manipulates not because he is a brat, but because one of his major tasks, as a child, is to test things about the world. One of the jobs of parenting is to show the limits of how things work in a social world.

FATHER'S ROLE

Despite the efforts of feminists and others to equalize parental roles, I still hear mothers complaining that fathers are not involved enough with their kids. Many fathers do not realize how important their role is. Only when your kid can throw a fast ball right over the plate, and has a great breaking curve, do you perk up. A father can learn to be as interested and empathetic as the mother.

Also, your role as father needs to be one of consistency. Storm troopers, who intervene only at the last desperate moment, do more harm than good. Women are attempting to get men involved in all aspects of parenting. Paternal involvement is more important than ever now that many more women are working. Women are sharing the work load equally but are not sharing the parenting equally.

Many fathers need to reexamine how important they can be to their young children. I've seen fathers who are responsive and empathetic with their children at a very early age. On the other hand, many fathers express sentiments like, "I don't understand why my child always goes to my wife when he wants to talk." These fathers are very poor observers of their own behavior. The lack of involvement actually cues the child that the father is not available.

Sometimes mothers inadvertently sabotage a father's involvement by criticizing his handling of the children. Many fathers back off. In this instance, the mother is conveying the feeling that she is the only one capable of handling a problem. I want to point this out in order to not present a one-sided view.

Many fathers really do care. Frequently men grow up deficient in their experience with children. They don't know how to be involved. A father's participation helps a child learn what men are all about, what they have to offer, and what they can give in return for a deeper experience. A father must realize his importance to his children and take it seriously.

PART II
BEHAVIOR
IN THE HOME

4

Daily Routines

MORNING BEHAVIOR

We must first understand what "morning" means to an adult and what "morning" means to a child. You presume your child understands what she should do the moment you shout, "It's time to get up!" "Get dressed and brush your teeth." "Get ready for school." This is your agenda, and you want your child to simply understand what is expected of her. You are in a rush. She should understand. No way!

Your child's agenda is to lounge in bed as long as she feels like it, get up when and if she's ready, play in her room, watch television, and then snap her fingers for you to fix her breakfast. Maybe, if she feels like it, she'll go to school. If she doesn't feel like it, she'll just stay home and play. Does this mean your kid is being a brat or a monster? No. Your child is performing the tasks she thinks are important. Now do you see why there is a conflict of wills? Again, it relates to the difference in agendas.

Your child is sure you're crazy for running around, screaming and rushing, and telling her she needs to get dressed. Statements like, "You won't grow big and strong if you don't eat your breakfast," don't even make an impression on her. She thinks you are nuts! She doesn't need to get dressed, she doesn't care if she is late. If she's late, it embarrasses you more than it does her—in most cases. And growing up big and strong? She can take it or leave it.

Now we've defined the conflict. What do we do?

First Step

Stop screaming from the other room, "Get ready or you're going to be late!" Stop giving warnings. Instead, set up a simple, consistent structure ahead of time. If you've been inconsistent with this issue in the past, this is the time to remember the speech about how you and your child are going to do things differently.

Second Step

Tell your child that her first jobs upon arising are getting dressed, brushing teeth, and getting to the table. No television, no playing, no messing around. Take the time to see that it is done—even if you have to stand over her. Don't say, "Why aren't you getting dressed?" Instead say, "I'm going to help you get started. If you can't follow the rules, you will miss TV this morning or you will have no playtime." Remember, the consequence depends upon your child.

If your child won't dress herself, help her get started by putting on her clothing. Then show her you can make her get dressed, no matter what she does, even if she's screaming and yelling. Some young children will resist to the point that it seems physically impossible for you to get them out of pajamas and into school clothes. If your child persists in making the morning difficult for you, let her know she is losing more television time. Believe me, "helping" your child until she is actually ready is more efficient than yelling from the kitchen, nineteen times, while scrambling eggs.

Third Step

Refuse to listen to arguments. At the hint of any argument, just repeat, "It's time to get dressed (or brush your teeth) now. I know it is hard to listen, but this is the only thing we are going to concentrate on until we are done." Being a good observer means noticing that you only say this. Don't babble on about all your frustrations, and don't continue asking why in the world she isn't getting dressed. *Don't argue with her.*

Fourth Step

Tell your child that if she isn't ready by the time you are ready to leave, she will have to finish dressing in the car. Tell her if she doesn't get ready, she will miss breakfast as well. (She won't die, she'll just be hungry one morning in school.) You should also tell her that you hope she won't have to miss her television time or playtime later on.

Fifth Step

Tell your child that you really hope both of you can learn to get through the morning better. You will try, and you believe she can do better, too. This is reinforcing your belief in your child's potential to do better.

MEALTIME BEHAVIOR

Mealtime with many young children sometimes borders on disaster. Your reason for having a meal is to eat, drink, and be merry! (And maybe even teach your child some table manners!) This is your time to finally get a chance to sit down, relax, and talk. Ha! Ha!

If your kid messes with her food, gets up and down, argues with siblings, constantly chatters, perhaps punches her sister or brother in the nose to get your full attention, try to realize that her agenda is different than yours. She is testing limits and trying to make the experience of mealtime interesting. You are setting limits by attempting to get things done as quietly and as quickly as possible.

When your child has carried her "investigations" too far, you restore calm by using the following techniques.

First Step

Tell your child, no more than two times, "No more arguing or messing around." If she can't control herself, she will have to leave the table until she is ready to try again.

Second Step

Ask her to leave the table and return when she has gained control of herself. Some children need to be sent to their rooms, because they will continue acting too wild or silly even if they aren't at the table.

Third Step

Wait about five minutes and then ask your child (either from her room or wherever she is) if she'd like to try again. If she says, "Yes," she can come back to the table. Sometimes your child might start this behavior over again. In this case you should tell her, "I guess you are not ready to control yourself. You have to leave the room until the end of the meal."

For your child, leaving the room might not be enough. She might just enjoy herself in another part of the house. She might also let out some hair-raising screams that make it impossible for you to enjoy your meal—with or without her at the table. Remember, you have observed, and you know which consequences are important.

Tell your child that she has to leave the room, and when mealtime is over there will be nothing to eat until the next meal. This may be hard for some parents to do. I guarantee, though, that 99 percent of the parents reading this book are not starving their children to death.

Fourth Step

Approach your child the next day and say very positively (without acting angry), "I really hope you can remember the rules so I won't have to send you away from the table. I believe that you can learn to follow these rules."

If you follow these procedures immediately and consistently, you decrease your own stress because you know that each time your child's behavior is disruptive, you now have a system that works. If the procedures are to be effective, you have to follow them only a few times to demonstrate to your child that you are in complete control of mealtime behavior.

TELEPHONE BEHAVIOR

Sometimes it seems that the devil controls your child the moment the phone rings and you answer it. She may have been playing quietly in her room. She may not have even wanted to be with you. However, as soon as your attention is focused on talking to a friend (and potentially on her), she's wild, pulling and tugging at your sleeve, screaming for food, potty, or whatever.

Parents tend to make unrealistic statements like, "I'll be off in a minute," or, "This is an important long distance call!" or "Don't you know I'm talking to the doctor? Be quiet!" When you speak like this to your child, you are not being honest with her. Most children learn very early that most calls aren't nearly as critical as you make them sound. By not observing your behavior, you confuse the issue. You are not helping your child learn that you have a right to be on the telephone whenever you wish. It makes no difference if you are chatting to a friend about after-Christmas sales or planning a fishing trip.

When you are on the telephone, your child is aware that she doesn't have your undivided attention. She likes to think you are there just for her any moment of the day or night. She doesn't care what is important to you, and she may not be old enough to care. But you must teach her that she can't interrupt you when you're on the telephone.

First Step

Tell your child there is going to be a new rule when you are on the telephone. Tell her "Sometimes I need to be left alone when I am on the phone. I know it's hard for you to leave me alone when I'm talking."

Second Step

Verbalize to her that, if she cannot leave you alone while you're on the telephone, you are going to send her to her room. Now, how are you going to manage to do this while you're on the telephone?

Third Step

Show her that you will hang up *any* phone call and put her in her room if she won't listen. Show your child that dealing with her inappropriate behavior is more important than the telephone call. She may think she is winning when you are forced to stop talking. But remember that the most important discipline for your child is taking the pleasure away from her! So you send her to her room. If you consistently follow through with this method, at some point your child will see that bothering you when you are on the phone is not worth it.

An alternate approach works for a young child (three to six). Tell her to come and set up an activity next to you while you are talking (if the conversation is one your child may listen to). Say in a very positive way, "I'd like you in here with me. Why don't you work on your coloring book?" The message is, "I want to be with you." This might not work, unfortunately, when the phone rings for you and your caller can't wait for you to organize paper dolls and finger paints!

Part of the discussion with your child might include some agreement about an activity she could engage in while you are on the phone. If she wants to be near you at such times, she will have to choose a feasible activity, such as drawing or cutouts.

Remember—your child's behavior is based on her agenda. She thinks her survival is contingent on having your undivided attention at all times. Your agenda is to reassure her, and at the same time to assert yourself and teach appropriate behavior.

CHORES

Some children refer to this as "slave labor." You probably view it as a way for your child to learn responsibility at an early age. This isn't a bad idea. Parents who are not observant simply want their kids to automatically clean up their mess, even though Dad's garage looks like the aftermath of the Vietnam War and Mom's closet looks like it was in the path of Hurricane Cindy. This is setting poor standards on the parent's part.

However, many parents still have the magical idea that all you have to do is tell your child to make her bed and it will be made. From your child's point of view, chores have very little meaning. She cares little about comments such as, "If you don't learn to pick things up now, you'll grow up to be a slob" or "How are you ever going to learn to take care of yourself?" Your three-year-old stares at you and thinks, "Man, this person is weird. What's all this taking care of yourself stuff?"

If you haven't been locked into a struggle, the first thing to do is start your child with a few daily tasks, even as early as age two. This will instill in her a feeling that the chores are part of her daily routine. If your attitude is positive and fun, not matter-of-fact, she will learn that it is rewarding to share tasks with you.

Since many of you are locked into a pattern of negative behavior, you will probably get resistance to this approach. Let's discuss what to do to overcome the problem.

First Step

Tell your child you're going to stop yelling and arguing about daily tasks. From now on, tell her you will pick out chores she is expected to do every day—usually no more than two to four. Don't broach this subject like an army sergeant; rather do it in a firm, warm way. Tell her that both of you will decide when the work will be done. If you are unable to agree upon a time, tell her that you are the parent, and you will decide. If you've been struggling, this may very well be the first argument your child will present.

Second Step

Decide what your follow-through technique will be. Typically, parents yell, "Did you clean up your room yet?" "Did you feed the dog?" Your child will probably say, "Yes!" But when you go into the dog's area and find Fido yapping from hunger, you stomp into your child's room and demand, "Why did you lie to me?" This is not good follow-through.

You might have to say, "It's time to feed the dog now," and follow your child around to see that she does it. Don't let anything divert her. As you follow her around, don't mumble, "Why do I have to follow you around? Why can't you just clean your room when I tell you?" Just see that she does it. If you have to say something, simply say, "I know you don't want to clean up now because it's hard, but let's get it finished." Now, parents, I mean grit your teeth if necessary and say no more, no matter what your child says.

Third Step

Continue following her around to see that she finishes her chores until she can do them alone. This should be necessary only the first few times. It is important that she know you're going to make sure she finishes. She will know you are in control.

Your child may come up with statements like, "Please give me some time," or "Why do I have to do it now?" Your job as a good observer is not to listen to any comments. Put cotton, corks, or anything in your ears and just see that she follows your instructions. Reinforce this by telling her, "I'm glad to see you are finally listening to me," even though she might be barely cooperating. The idea is to establish a positive reaction.

Instead of bombarding your child with the fact that it's time to do her chores, you might tell her to pick up her toys a few minutes in advance. Try to put yourself in your child's place. How would you like it if your spouse or boss walked in and demanded, "I want you to pick up those papers now!" You'd probably get angry and rebel, right? On the other hand, if she said, "Gee, I'd sure appreciate it if you would pick up those papers the way we had decided," you would respond differently.

Fourth Step

Tell your child that if she continues to resist doing her chores, there will be a consequence. Remember, this is after you have tried the preceding steps for a few weeks, including all my suggestions.

For example, you would say, "From now on, unless you can follow my rules without making such a fuss, you will have to go to bed early . . . or you will lose television time . . . or there will be no story at bedtime."

If you are clear about establishing chores for your child, you must have structure, follow-through, and consequences. This is important, especially if your child resists in a very strong and negative way.

BEDTIME

Wouldn't it be great if you could just get your kid to bed by saying, "You need your rest" and "You know how crabby you are in the morning when you don't get enough sleep." Again, this is your agenda and as we know by now, your agenda means very little to your child. She's saying to herself, "You're crazy. I don't need my rest and I don't think I'm crabby in the morning!" She knows about her fear of separation from you and her anxiety about being alone in the dark. There is also a lot of activity going on in the living room, and the kitchen—anywhere adults are. She doesn't understand why she can't be a part of it. So she comes out of her room about nineteen times for a drink of water or wanders into the bathroom . . . or she has to tell you a deep, dark secret. She might tell you, as a last resort, that she needs you and loves you very much, and she must be with you. In the meantime, after she emerges from her room for the fourth time, you're almost ready to hide in the closet so she won't find you.

You probably wonder why comments like these don't inspire your child to go into her room and go to sleep. "You come out of that room one more time and you'll never get out again!" or "Why aren't you asleep yet?" or "Didn't I already tell you that you've been to the bathroom enough?"

Again, is it because she's trying to ruin your life? Or, is she simply telling you that it's really hard to go to bed when she'd rather be up with you? Do you ever verbalize your understanding of these feelings to your child? Sometimes it might help just to acknowledge those sentiments. Now you understand the dilemma. So what do you do about it?

First Step

Establish a definite bedtime, allowing approximately half an hour to unwind and get ready. You must individualize this for your child. Let her know the same time each night that it is time to prepare for bed. Included in this new approach should be a warning that the typical ninety-seven drinks of water, the five trips to the bathroom, and the deep, dark secrets she must tell you after she's been tucked into bed are not allowed. Tell her that starting the next night, all requests for water, bathroom trips, kisses, and so forth must be out of the way as soon as she is in bed. When she is in bed, that is the end of the bedtime routine.

This means the scenario stops. No more typical responses like, "I thought you just went to the bathroom," "I already gave you a kiss," or, "You're going to drown if you have any more water."

Second Step

Do not respond to her beyond one comment. If she calls you fifty times, screams, cries, or begs, just say, "I know you don't feel like going to bed, but I'm not going to answer any more questions. I've already told you the rules. Good night." You could add, "I love you."

After that one statement you would love it if she would just stop crying or calling you and fall asleep. Most children will not say, "I guess there are new rules, and I'll just go to sleep instead of creating my normal ruckus." If your child thought you would stick to these new rules, she might fall asleep. She is probably convinced, however, that you don't mean business. If you have been struggling with this issue, she will assume she can keep the dialogue going between you.

Third Step

Be prepared if she decides to investigate why you are so silent. She might come out of her room just to make sure this silent home is really hers. If this happens, don't yell out to her, "Get back in there. Didn't I already tell you to get in that bed?" As calmly as you can, take your child back to her room and tell her if she comes out again, she'll go to bed fifteen minutes earlier the next night. Give her one chance.

Your child may test you many times. You may have to show her that you will increase the consequence fifteen minutes each time. If she's a very young child (two or three) you might want to make it five minutes each time. If she has been very resistant in the past, she may be in for some very early bedtimes for a while.

Fourth Step

Take this step in extreme cases when your child keeps testing you. She comes out of her room time and again, no matter what the consequences are. *You must show her that you will stand by the door and hold it or sit there in order to keep her in her room.* Now, this is not comfortable for some parents, but some children may test you that far. Your child is thinking, "They don't mean this. They'll give in. How long do they think they can hold out? That dummy isn't going to sit by that door because I know her favorite television show is coming on in a minute!"

The point is, even if you are about to miss your favorite program, you have to demonstrate to your child that you are not going to give in. It is much better for you (as strange as it may seem or as undesirable as it may be) to stand and hold the door, than it is to become so enraged that you feel like buzz bombing the kid's room.

Fifth Step

Follow through the next day. Whether your child acts like an angel or pretends you are ruining her life, you tell her that even though she had a hard time last night, these are the new rules. You know it's going to be difficult but you hope she won't have to go to bed early again that night. Tell her you know she can learn to follow these new rules.

Remember, convey this in the best way you can, even though you may not have felt marvelous about the struggle the evening before. This is another example of changing something negative into something positive.

Sixth Step

This step applies if you followed the procedures but blew your stack in the process. Just tell your child, "I'm glad you finally listened to me about bedtime. Next time I'll try not to scream and yell. But I hope you can follow the rules better."

SPECIAL TIME

Since most parents, regardless of their very busy lives, do a great deal for their children, they have difficulty understanding why their children nag them for more of their time. Your usual comments are, "Just a minute," "Sometime," "Later"—the famous little phrases that your child would like to murder you for. These comments really mean, "Don't bug me, kid." "I probably won't play with you, anyway." Later, as she gets older, your child will say to you, "You never played with me," or "You never did anything with me," and you will probably feel guilty. In order to avoid this trap, I would suggest the following.

A child responds to structure. She feels secure knowing she can count on certain rituals. If you provide a half hour once a week or a regular time each night (when your schedule permits) to be with your child, you let her know there is a time and a place to connect and have fun together. Let her know that she can do what she wants—play games, read, or whatever. This time will not be taken away from her. If you allow your child to do what she wants to do (and I don't mean going to Disneyland—just simple at-home activities) you are giving her constructive, meaningful control of "special time." You guarantee that your child can be with you in her own special way.

If you decide to play games with your child, it is important to make every effort not to act bored, disinterested, or competitive about who wins. Your attitude about this "special time" together is very important. This may sound boring to a parent, but it has particular significance to your child. Later she may not remember these special times as special unless you have shown her they are special to you as well.

Scheduling special time allows your child to get your attention without driving you crazy, making faces, running amok, or tackling you in a dark hallway. If you are having a difficult day and you remind her (who is trying desperately to get your attention) "Remember, we're going to have our special time this afternoon," you are focusing on her needs. She should be told that she will have your undivided attention later.

If your positive efforts to meet her needs do not control behavior, follow with a consequence. Tell your child, "If you can't listen to me now, you're going to lose your special time today." If you are locked in and misbehavior is persistent, sometimes taking away the special time is necessary. It shows your child that her inappropriate behavior is the important issue. If you are a good observer and pick the right consequence, you will only have to do this a few times before her behavior improves.

Since special time can be a positive experience for you and your child, consider using this consequence only if others have been ineffective.

TELEVISION

Is it a monster or a godsend? For the last thirty years, the phenomenon of television has left most parents confused, anxious, and concerned (though some are secretly relieved that the "daily companion" keeps their children busy). Should television be a babysitter, educator, or pleasurable experience? It can be any of these things. Frequently, though, it is a place where children tune out the world—just as adults do.

Many parents spend hours watching the tube. It is therefore pretty hard to keep children from watching it. The child sees people getting maimed, killed, bopped on the head, laughed at, and scared out of their wits. In the case of cartoons, these characters spring back to life in the next frame—unscathed. Most kids can survive and enjoy the experience. Many children, though, feel anxious as a result of the confusing messages. This is particularly true for very young children—from two to five.

Most parents are not able to eliminate television totally. The next best step, then, is to take time to monitor your child's viewing. You should sit down with her and talk about the parts of a story that help communicate an important idea. A sensitive and poignant story can help a child feel comfortable with her feelings. At times television can be a vehicle to open up communication between you and your child. Without supervision of viewing time, she will grow up thinking that the world is a very strange place. It's morbid, oversentimental, and confusing. If she watches soap operas, she learns that it takes two years before you finally tell someone you're hurt, that you have to discuss divorce or separation with fifty-two people before you tell your spouse.

If you have been fighting about how much time your child spends in front of the television, you must begin to unlock the struggle.

First Step

Restructure the use of your television. Begin by defining specific times when your child may watch. Sit down with her and explain the new schedule by saying, "Since we fight so much over your use of television, we are going to have new rules. You might not feel good about some of them, but you need to learn to follow my rules about watching TV." Tell her there will be a specific time for television that will fit your family's routine. When you tell her it's time to stop, you expect her to listen.

Second Step

(Why can't it ever stop at Step One?) Stop yelling, "Turn that darn TV off! You never listen to me!" Walk in and show your child that you have control of the television and that you will turn it off. Tell her that you will continue turning it off if she doesn't listen to you. If she can turn it off herself, you will not come in and do it for her. Again, you are telling your child and showing her that you have control of the situation. And you are saying that she can have responsible, constructive control when she is ready.

Third Step

This is the consequence. Let your child know that if she cannot listen to you, there will be no television viewing the next day. If she waits until you're talking on the phone or in the shower to sneak a few peeks at her favorite show, let her know she will continue to lose viewing time.

Remember, do not make unrealistic statements. Don't say, "OK, that's it! No television for two weeks!" You want to give your child a chance to redeem her control by following your rules.

Give systematic consequences. If your child continues to disobey, tell her in advance that the next time she is disobedient she will lose two days of television instead of one. She will finally realize that a "no win" situation exists for her and will probably decide to follow the rules.

Remember, once you establish the guidelines, there is no discussion, no argument. You do not become the overtalker. You do not lecture about the evils of television or about the virtues of children doing creative, active projects. Any kid will tune out. If you told your child ahead of time what the rules were, and you've observed your own behavior and made the consequences clear, you need only to follow through.

HOMEWORK

A six-year-old is not usually informed that her job for the next twelve years, come rain, sleet, or snow, is homework, and that she must complete it whether she wants to or not, even if it's hard, boring, or monotonous.

You probably started her career by saying, "Oh, look at all those nice spelling words. You did such a good job!" This slowly degenerates into, "Oh, that's nice." Finally, your kid says, "Look what I did!" and all she gets is, "Uh huh." When she gets older, your comment on the subject is, "Do your homework!"

Your agenda is for her to learn very early to sit down at a regular time and diligently do her homework. She should demonstrate enthusiasm and excitement while engrossed in her studies. The reality is that you look over and your kid has one leg hanging over her desk, and is chewing her pencil with her head in the clouds. You will probably feel like screaming, "You're not concentrating. If you don't learn to do homework now, you will have a hard time in high school!" This is an anxiety-provoking comment and induces fear in your kid. She's not interested in anything that far in the future.

Around the time of first grade, children should have structure and organization for doing their homework. Before this time, homework assignments are rarely given. Children should experience school as an interesting, enjoyable place that gives them learning pleasure. This includes interacting and cooperating with others, following directions, and developing normal curiosities. Don't project your anxieties into the future and think that if your child isn't doing her homework willingly, it means she won't be able to attend Harvard or MIT. In other words, her life won't be ruined if she needs help with her homework habits.

The important issue is to make your child comfortable about learning. Be clear about your expectations and set up a realistic structure for homework. Some children—and you're lucky if you have one of them—do their homework without much prodding, and they know how to organize their study time. However, this seems atypical.

First Step

Examine your own attitude. If you are the kind of parent who can sit down calmly and make the homework experience a positive one, you will make your child feel comfortable. If you are tense, a perfectionist, impatient, or easily frustrated, stay away from your child and her homework. She has a right to make mistakes and daydream.

If you are lucky enough to have a spouse who is patient and therefore more capable, the effective parent should work with the child.

Sometimes neither parent is effective. In this case, you must keep in touch with the school in order to know what is expected of your child. Children don't always tell you! You must develop a positive contact with the teacher. Ask her to tell you when your child needs extra help. Surprisingly, if you keep in touch with the teacher and you are persistent, you can learn what the school offers for children who are having problems. Most children only need a little help with the discipline of homework.

Second Step

Establish a designated time for homework. This will depend on your child. You have to be a good observer. It may be best for her to do her homework before playtime, or she might do it more comfortably in the evening. If your child is six, she is not going to have excessive homework, and it is best to get it out of the way. If she has television time at night, you could establish the rule that homework must be done before she watches television.

Third Step

Stop asking questions like, "Did you do your homework?" If she answers, "Yes," don't say, "Oh yeah, what did you do?" If she says, "I don't know," don't respond, "What do you mean, you don't know?"

It is unrealistic to expect your child to monitor herself. If you suspect trouble, contact the school to find out whether or not she is keeping up with the homework. Do not accuse her of lying. Do not ask, "Why didn't you tell me the truth about your homework?" Your child's agenda is to get out of doing homework so she can do something more interesting instead. In this situation you should comment, "I guess you didn't tell me you had homework because you didn't want to do it. I am going to work something out with your teacher so I can help you learn to follow through with your homework. However, if you find it hard to tell me the truth about what work you have to do, I will have to limit your playtime when I find out you are having difficulty. I hope you can tell me the truth so you don't lose the time you have for fun."

Set up a time to talk with the teacher every week to determine what schoolwork has been assigned. This information may clash with the claims your child makes!

Initially this will seem like extra work. But it will take less energy than driving yourself nuts and being angry because your child didn't tell you. Once you have established a routine, she knows that you are going to find out the truth one way or another. Additionally, there will be a consequence if she doesn't tell the truth. If you apply your routine in a matter-of-fact way, you won't make home-work a loaded issue.

Fourth Step

Quit arguing with your child. Don't tell her that her life is in jeop-ardy until her homework is done. Establish the structure, then fol-low through with a consequence. If your child doesn't do her homework, tell her she won't be able to play, or she will have no television time. Being a good observer, you know which conse-quence is meaningful to her.

Fifth Step

If necessary, sit down with your child (if she is young) and help her with her homework. Allow her to experience homework as a plea-surable activity with you. After that, set up a slow but consistent withdrawal structure until, she gradually becomes more autono-mous. After the first month of doing homework with your child (if you are still sane), prepare her by saying: "Now this time I want you to do this page alone, since you have been doing such a good job. I'll be in the kitchen. You can sit here at the table and finish that page. Then I want you to show it to me when you're done, because I am still very interested." You can add that you will be close by if she needs help.

It is most important to create a good attitude toward homework. When a child learns that she has a job to do day in and day out for the next twelve years, she often feels ambivalence, frustration, and anxiety. We don't give children much emotional support in this area. Reassure her and tell her what is expected. Do not give her decision-making power.

Your child will have the option of doing her homework or losing a pleasurable experience. Do not engage in battle. Simply take control. Remember, if you have a consequence, you are relieved of the struggle.

5

Getting Along with Others

COMPANY IN THE HOME

An evening with the Joneses—at least to your child—is probably one of the most dreaded events possible. When the Joneses are expected to invade your household, your child hears all your famous comments like, "Now, Mr. and Mrs. Jones are coming over. If you don't behave I'll kill you!"

Your agenda is to have a nice, comfortable evening with your child looking adorable, the entire family a candidate for Family of the Year. All this preparation and anxiety is to impress the Joneses so that when they leave they'll say, "My, aren't they just the nicest family . . . and that wonderful child of theirs. So well behaved!" Well, ladies and gentlemen, we are about to destroy another fantasy.

Your child is thinking, "Boy, not them again. The last time they showed up, I wasn't even allowed to blink. I'm going to have to listen to that Mr. Jones, who keeps patting me on the shoulder and telling me how big I've grown."

Usually you pump your child with warnings on how to behave, what to do, and what not to do. These pronouncements tell him that he should act like an adult rather than a kid. It also shows that you are more concerned about the Joneses' perception of your family than what the experience means to your child. This is not to say that he should be allowed to run around like a maniac, nor am I suggesting that he should do anything he wants. But it is important to show your child that he is basically acceptable the way he is. If you ask him to be drastically different all of a sudden, you are telling him he is not OK. That isn't your intention, but that is the message he receives when he picks up your anxiety about company.

Your warnings mean that you are nervous and you want the evening to go well. If you express your feelings to your child, you have a chance to tell him there is nothing wrong with him. You are also not predicting that he will act up. You may even find out that his behavior will improve because he wants to support you.

You must understand how your child experiences visitors. If they are people he likes, or if they are good with kids, your child will want a lot of attention. If he hasn't seen the visitors in a while, he will want even more attention, just as you would. You may find yourself in competition with your child for center attraction!

If the guests do not relate well to children and you ask your kid to be delightful, warm, and open after he has received a sour half-smile and a perfunctory handshake, you're asking too much. You can't ask more from your four-year-old than what "mature" adults are prepared to give. Don't be surprised if your child greets such a visitor sullenly. If he drops his head and runs out of the room, if he emerges from time to time, peeking around corners and giving the undesired intruder the evil eye, this should not astonish you.

You might be anxious about unfavorable gossip being spread about your "unruly" child. You might be cringing and thinking, "Just wait until the Joneses leave. That kid's going to get it! After everything I told him, he still can't behave!"

Some of you out there are probably saying, "Peeking in and out of the room? Spying? Eyeing the guest suspiciously? Is this guy kidding? If that's all my kid did, there wouldn't be any problem." Let's look at the typical parental reaction when a child runs into a room where there are visitors, interrupts conversation, yanks at your clothes, and screams, "Daddy, Daddy, I need help!" You probably grit your teeth and glare, hoping to communicate by burning a hole in his brain. Then you add, "Not now, can't you see I'm talking?" If your child is typical, he'll probably persist and ask loudly, "When are they leaving anyway? You said they wouldn't be here that long!" Now you're ready to crawl under the sofa. You want to play the storm trooper, but then guests would think the whole family is crazy. You are sure they're already thinking, "Boy, does that kid get away with murder. They don't have an ounce of control over him."

First Step

Prepare your child for visitors. I don't mean with the usual warnings and anxiety-provoking statements. Tell him that none of the rules change just because there is company and that when you ask him to do something, you expect him to do it even if there are visitors. If you've dropped the rules when visitors come or if you never made your expectations clear, now is the time to observe your own behavior.

Second Step

This step is necessary if your child continues to interrupt or bother your guests, despite your discussion with him about the rules for company. Then you must take the time to deal with the issue, even if it means leaving one partner alone with the guests for a while.

Let's say your child is shoving a stuffed animal into the face of your guest and demanding attention. Your reply, even if you feel awkward is, "Sometimes Johnny gets so excited when visitors are over that he doesn't notice when they are talking. He just wants to show the things that are important to him." You begin to clarify the issues to your child.

Then you say, "All right, Johnny, you can show our visitors two of your favorite toys, but then I expect you to go play in your room or watch television. If you have a hard time doing this, I'll have to help you follow the rule." If you say this firmly and non-critically, and you don't get embarrassed in front of other adults, you are demonstrating to your child that your expectations of him don't change in front of company. In addition, you are demonstrating to your visitors that you have control of the situation and you are not uncomfortable when your child has trouble adjusting to company.

Third Step

This step is for those persistent children who, despite these initial warnings, continue disruptive behavior. Excuse yourself, take your child out of earshot of the visitors and reinforce, in an understanding and firm way, what you established before your visitors arrived. You may ask your child to try one more time to follow the rules before you set a different limit. For instance, "Mom told you that if you don't listen to me about screaming and yelling when we have company, you will have to spend time in your room. I will give you one more try. If you do this again, you will just have to go to your room."

Fourth Step

This is the consequence the child must accept, such as going to his room. Since your priority must be to teach him, you say to your guests, "Excuse me, but it's important for Billy to learn that he must behave even when guests are over, so I have to take care of this right now." Even if it means taking fifteen minutes to teach him to stay in his room, he will learn that you follow through under special circumstances. This is really surprising to a child who does not think a parent will follow through with discipline in front of guests because of the embarrassment.

A SPECIAL ISSUE WITH GUESTS

Sometimes you inadvertantly trap your child when you have company. You might say, "Susie, why don't you show Mrs. Jones how beautifully you play your oboe?" Mrs. Jones looks somewhat bemused at the five-year-old who can hardly carry, let alone play, the cumbersome instrument. She says, "Oh, that's OK, she doesn't have to play it if she doesn't want to." Your child says, "Do I have to, Mommy?" You reply, "Yes, you play that one song so well!" Reluctantly, she gives in and brings out the oboe. With her head hanging down, she tries to play "Three Blind Mice" in barely audible tones. You are embarrassed and say, "Play louder, Susie!"

Coaxing her fuels this issue unnecessarily, making it a miserable experience for guest and child.

Please realize that a performance in front of guests might be awkward for your child. It is true that some children delight in performing and will come out with a complete brass band, happily playing for visitors for a straight hour. Many children, however, are shy about it.

If you sense that your child feels pressured by a suggestion to play her oboe or to sing a song, simply say, "I guess you're not in the mood and that's OK. Maybe you'll feel like it later." Don't be surprised when half an hour later, your kid marches in with the oboe blaring right in the middle of an adult conversation. She's had time to digest your request without pressure and decided that maybe it wouldn't be so bad to show off a little.

Again, the basic issue is to understand the difference between your agenda or expectations and what your child may feel about the same program. Try to remember your child's feelings. At the same time, be very clear about your own expectations and then follow through if your child is unable to comply with your request.

RELATIVES IN THE HOME

Many parents are confused to see that their parents are much more lenient with their grandchildren than they were with them as children. Your child knows that when the grandparents come over, he will receive lots of goodies and lots of attention. Why do grandparents undermine your efforts to maintain some structure and discipline?

Age tends to mellow and this accounts for some of the indulgence. Also, grandparents are not raising the child on a daily basis. They get tremendous gratification from your child's interest in them, and they don't concern themselves (too much) with the ongoing hard work of socialization. The ultimate responsibility for your child's development is yours. They just want to relax and enjoy him.

A well-meaning relative can really be disruptive. Some offer unsolicited suggestions. Others interfere with discipline. Suppose you are dealing with a problem and your mother says, "Gee, what's wrong? Can't he just have one more scoop of ice cream?" You think, "Why does she have to say these things now?" When you are dealing with your child, this type of response from your mother makes you feel sabotaged.

Baby-sitting grandparents can be the worst offenders. Many grandparents will simply defy your rules and sway your willing child by saying, "Don't tell your mom or your dad that I let you stay up." The next day you learn from your child that he was up until midnight.

Parents, grandparents, and children begin to feel angry, hurt, and bewildered. Let's examine the source of these conflicting feelings and conflicting agendas.

Your agenda is to keep things as consistent and orderly as possible, and you hope that this will be honored by your relatives. Your child's agenda is, "Oh boy! Grandma and Grandpa are coming over! I'm really going to get away with murder. It doesn't matter what Mom or Dad says, because I can talk Grandma or Grandpa into all kinds of things. All I have to do is act cute and needy, and they will give me anything!"

The grandparents' agenda is to enjoy a child without being fully responsible for his development, and to be seen as the most wonderful grandparents in the world. Their unconscious agenda may be, "I know how to handle that child better than my daughter/son does!"

First Step

Ask your parents in an understanding way whether or not they are comfortable following your rules. Tell them that your child has not been following the rules. Ask them if they can follow the rules you have set for him.

Some grandparents are unable to admit their discomfort. In that case, you simply say, "We are going to make it a special time for Johnny when you come over. We'll let him stay up when you are here, but we will let him know that he has to follow the regular rules once you are gone." This way both your feelings and those of the grandparents are being respected, and this prevents your child from taking advantage of the discord. Of course, if the grandparents take care of him every day or on a regular basis, fluctuating expectations would not work.

Second Step

Help your child understand ahead of time that when Grandma or Grandpa or any doting relative comes over, you are going to let them disregard the regular rules of the house while they are there because it is a special day. If necessary, you will let him have an extra scoop of ice cream, stay up a little later, or have some special privileges.

Third Step

Explain to your child that once Grandma or Grandpa has gone home, the regular rules will apply once more. By reinforcing this, you're telling him that your expectations haven't changed even though the rules are temporarily different. You are also showing him that he doesn't have to "pull" anything in order to get his way when relatives are around. The grandparents will benefit because the conflict between you and them can be avoided, and this will reduce a lot of potential stress.

Fourth Step

If after a number of attempts your child fails to return to your rules, tell him that unless he can control himself, you will have to keep the regular rules all the time. Tell Grandma or Grandpa that there won't be any special rules when they are visiting.

Fifth Step

You can let your child know that when you think he is ready to accept the regular rules and the special rules when relatives are visiting, you will give him a chance to try again.

Sixth Step

Let's say that Grandma continues to interfere. Use the same technique discussed in the chapter about interaction with spouses. Without gritting your teeth, say, "Grandma doesn't always accept our rules, and I guess she thinks we're being unfair, especially since she has difficulty not allowing you to have your own way all the time."

If the grandparent continues to contradict and undermine the parents, you need stronger ammunition.

Seventh Step

Say to your mother—very firmly—"This is something I feel I have to handle this way." Then tell your child—equally firmly—"Your grandmother and I don't agree about this, but these are the rules, and you have to follow them anyway."

Obviously, we are talking about relatives who basically have a good relationship with you and who would understand and accept your way of handling issues. If your family relationships are complex and your relatives rarely agree with you or will battle you for the control of your child, these suggestions will be of little value. But they do provide a way in which you can look at improving issues and possibly get better behavior from your child.

I do not want to oversimplify this area. Families are sometimes caught in very intricate webs of poor relationships because of differences in child-rearing attitudes. These problems can be very emotional. Parents and relatives may need professional help to learn how to institute the techniques and suggestions in this section. Until the struggle is unlocked, interactions with relatives will be difficult.

BABY-SITTERS

The baby-sitter issue is another example of adult agendas versus children's agendas. Your child's agenda is, "Why do they have to go out again when I need them at home?" or, "I want to go with them, and I feel scared when they're gone. If they think I'm going to make it easy for them when they leave, they're crazy. They're going to suffer good." The child's deeper wish is, "If I look like I'm falling apart and dying, maybe they won't go." When children reach adolescence, none of these problems exist—they will escort you out the door!

Your agenda is to have a change from your routine, particularly if you are a "nonworking" mother. You need to get out of the house to know that there is a world beyond car pools and Little League. But don't try to explain to your child how marvelous and necessary it is for you to get out of the house. He won't understand. To ask your child to appreciate your personal adult needs is to burden him with unnecessary responsibility.

Parents frequently avoid these issues. Some sneak out of the house, leaving the baby-sitter and child bewildered. Most parents feel anxious when their children are upset. There is nothing more disconcerting than starting the evening to the echo of a child's screams. It is understandable that parents try to avoid confronting the difficulty of leaving the house.

Another well-known tactic is bribery, involving promises of toys or candy at the last minute in order to help your child feel good about your leaving. Then you belatedly remember your promise at midnight and find yourself cruising around for an all-night drug store that carries purple-and-white teddy bears. If you don't have the toy by the time you reach home, you sneak in the door and pray that your child won't ask you about it the next morning. As you must know by now, they always remember.

This sneaky, guilt-ridden behavior tells your child that you're not very comfortable about leaving him. Children have a normal, deep-seated fear of abandonment. Young children—particularly between the ages of three and six—do not have enough life experience to say to themselves, "Oh, I know they will always return. There's nothing for me to worry about."

Children also worry about the loss of continuity. A child knows that when he needs something, Mom or Dad is available. Loss of this availability threatens security. He is afraid the baby-sitter won't know what to do.

Additionally, your child thinks you are going out to do some exciting things. He fears that he is missing something important. It is difficult for a child to think he is missing anything. You may tell him you are only having dinner with friends. In his fantasy you're at a fancy dress ball, without him.

Baby-sitters come in all shapes and sizes. They are a distinct phenomenon of the twentieth century. Some of them who take advantage are the ones you don't rehire. They raid the refrigerator, call long distance on the phone, and invite friends over. Others are mature and professional.

First Step

You must prepare your child for a baby-sitter, particularly if he has problems with separation. Have the baby-sitter come early to meet him, even if you need to spend extra money. The baby-sitter should always come in advance to meet your child. If it is not possible for the baby-sitter to meet him prior to baby-sitting, it would be helpful for the sitter to telephone in advance to say hello to him, to ask him what kind of games he likes to play, and to say that he or she is looking forward to meeting him. Describing your child's interests to the sitter will help to establish a comfortable rapport.

Second Step

Go over the rules for the evening with the baby-sitter and child. This does not mean comments like, "You be good now. Listen to Mary Jane so she'll come back sometime." Statements like this give your child the feeling of power or guilt. You might be praying silently that he will conduct himself decently so you won't be reduced to the bottom of the baby-sitter barrel, but don't let him think he controls the fate of the baby-sitter. Otherwise, he won't listen to Mary Jane, and you will never get out of the house.

Just repeat the rules to the baby-sitter in front of your child. If the child does not hear, you are giving him the opportunity to manipulate the sitter by saying things like, "Mommy said I could stay up until 9:00." The baby-sitter has to say, "She told me 8:00," and your child has the opportunity to start a dispute. Repeat the rules to both of them. Let the baby-sitter know that he or she can use you as a reinforcement. Assure the baby-sitter of your support and that you expect the rules to be followed.

Third Step

Prepare the baby-sitter for your child's potential reactions. Occasionally he will catch you off guard with comments at the door like, "Mommy, you told me the sitter wasn't old," or "I don't like her. I thought it would be the nice baby-sitter I had last week." Some sitters are not quite prepared for this, not to mention the parents, who feel like hiding behind the door. Instead of retreating, say something like, "Sometimes when Johnny doesn't know somebody, he says things like that. I think he's a little nervous because he doesn't know you."

If your child is prone to negative remarks, it might be a good idea to tell the baby-sitter. Say very bluntly, "My child might say things like 'I don't like you' just because he doesn't want us to leave." Perhaps you are worried that if you are this honest on the telephone, the sitter will decline to work for you. But a baby-sitter who personalizes a child's comments probably isn't the right sitter anyway. Most people know that it is not unusual for a child to respond in a negative way because of his discomfort. The sitter would rather know what to expect than to be bombarded with an impertinent greeting. This forthright approach also cures the child who thinks that if he can't get you to stay home, he can at least embarrass you with his comments.

Fourth Step

Apply a consequence if your child continues inappropriate behavior. First, tell him that even though he misbehaved, it is not going to stop you from going out. If he can't show better control, there will be a consequence the next day.

You must follow through. Remind your child that he didn't follow your rules. Even if he is very young, you should still enforce a minimum consequence. It is difficult for a two-year-old child, because he may have a hard time understanding a consequence that wasn't initiated immediately. But you should remind your young child that he couldn't go out and play because he didn't listen to the baby-sitter. An older child will understand this easily.

An exception to the fourth step involves the sitter who is good to your child but is unable to set limits or follow through with your rules. In this case, as we discussed previously about relatives, it is not fair to use a consequence.

This does not mean your child can go crazy just because he has a baby-sitter who is an ineffective disciplinarian. You should tell him, as you did in the case of your relative, that because you are going out, there will be special rules. He can stay up half an hour or an hour later than usual and watch television. These are the rules only for that night, and this does not indicate a change from your normal expectations of the rules. It is impossible to ask your child to have perfect control so that when you're not there, he internalizes and automatically obeys your rules even with an indulgent adult. By being this flexible, you are also being realistic about the strength of your baby-sitter.

Remember, it is common for children to test new teachers, friends, and baby-sitters, in order to understand what different people expect. By the way, adults do the same thing, in a seemingly more sophisticated fashion.

SIBLING BEHAVIOR

As a parent, you may frequently be caught in the middle of your children's fights. You probably ask yourself, "Why me?" You constantly scream things like, "If you don't stop all that fighting, I'm going to kill both of you!" ... "How can you do this to me when I'm such a good parent?" ... "Mrs. Jones's kids don't behave this way. How come you kids are so bad?"

These comments may temporarily relieve your initial frustrations. They will not evoke better behavior from your children.

Why do children constantly bicker and disagree? Because it's normal! One minute children hate one another; the next minute they like one another. Mixed feelings are a natural part of the growth process.

Much learning takes place when your children argue with each other. When they negotiate, they learn to master social situations.

They learn how it feels to lose or win. Shockingly, sometimes they even learn how to get along cooperatively.

As you listen to children bicker and scream, you may have a hard time believing that they are really learning. Your job is to help your children clarify what is happening. Be observant and you will determine what your children could possibly learn from this situation.

First Step

Know when the fighting has gone too far. "Far"—to me—is more than five minutes. As a general rule, if you watch your children argue, you'll see that usually it is brief. One or the other will probably give in. One will pout, the other will say, "I'm never going to play with you again!" Then, within a few minutes, they are back together again. Give your children a few minutes to deal with the problem themselves.

After about five minutes, tell them they are out of control and you will help them settle their dispute once they have regained control. This means that they should stop arguing about whose fault it is. Your children will probably respond immediately by telling you that you're being unfair or mean. Tell them that the only thing you're concerned about is that they're not controlling their behavior. When making this point, don't bring up other issues. Repeat that if they want to play together they must regain control.

Second Step

If they can't regain control, you must separate them. Give them five minutes to think about the problem. They may try to get together again in a few minutes. If one child chooses not to try again, your job as a parent is to relay that decision to the other child. Empathize with the child who wants to play. Tell him you know it's hard that his brother or sister doesn't want to play with him. Until they have both made up their minds to play together, they will have to play separately.

When children squabble, 90 percent of the time it is impossible for you to become an investigator or a crime fighter and get to the bottom of who really did what. Therefore, the real issue is to teach your children that they must learn to control themselves and get along. They must learn that there are limits to their behavior, and that you cannot be maneuvered and caught in the middle of an argument.

Third Step

Remain calm if your children don't get along immediately. If you've waited the token five minutes (remember to increase this if five minutes doesn't mean enough to them) and if they still haven't resolved the situation, go into the room and tell them to stop. Do not scream from the other room. Do not threaten nineteen times and fail to follow through. Give the children the option of coming to you to ask if they can play alone instead of arguing with each other. If the children refuse to follow your expectations, both will be punished. Emphasize that you will not take sides. You will defend their right to play without too much fighting. Frequently one child will play the victim. He'll attempt to continue the argument with statements like, "He's mean. He won't ever play with me." You simply repeat that he must respect his brother's right to play alone. No matter how difficult it is, he must learn to get along.

Give your children a chance to see that you have a systematic way of dealing with their fights. Once they learn that you can't be maneuvered and caught in the middle of the dispute, their behavior should improve.

Fourth Step

Sometimes a positive method can teach children to get along with each other. This would include playing games with them to teach them the skill of getting along. When using this special technique, tell them, "I will play some games with you to help you learn to get along." When they are getting along say to them, "See, you really can play well together." When a conflict erupts during a game, say to them, "Now we must find a way to stop the argument before we can continue playing the game." If either child stops arguing, you should say, "You really helped solve the problem, I am proud of you."

After a while and before you leave the room, tell them, "I want to see how well you play together when I leave the room, and if you do play well, I will play another game with you."

If your children still don't get along, do not yell things like, "Stop trying to cheat Johnny," or, "I'm not going to play any more if you can't get along," or, "You kids are impossible!" Simply say, "Unless you can play together without both of you getting so upset, we will have to stop and try later."

So far we've discussed techniques for staying out of the middle. However, if you definitely see one child taking advantage, you must adopt other measures. Don't tell the child who is taking advantage, "I see what you're doing. You're being mean to your brother," or "I told you over and over not to play with him like that. Your brother's going to grow up to hate you." The bully may act humble, but he's likely to hit his brother in the nose later.

Do not yell from the other room, "Johnny, are you being mean to your brother again?" Stick to what you actually see. The parent who is observant will come in and say, "Johnny, I see that you are having trouble controlling yourself. If you can't play with your brother without being so bossy or upset, you'll have to go to your room and think about it. When you're ready to come out, you may try again or you may play alone."

Now, it is typical for a child to say to you, "You always take his side and tell me that I'm wrong! It's not fair! He hit me first!" This is when it is important to be a good observer and realize that sometimes children are fairly equal in instigating conflict. If your child responds to you in this manner, say, "I know you feel that way, but sometimes you start things and sometimes your brother does, so I am going to help you get along better."

Constant sibling bickering can cause parents considerable stress. Resolving this issue may require hard work. Observe your own behavior. Do not become "used to" their bickering. If you truly want to change your children's behavior, realize that this will take time and that this is normal. Your role is to teach them that life is more fun when people get along.

SIBLING BEHAVIOR WITH VISITING FRIENDS

When his friends visit, your child's behavior may become dramatically different. Some children overcontrol, refusing to share toys. Some refuse to include siblings. Others tease, taunt, or become tyrannical.

You may become so embarrassed and infuriated that you are forced to intervene. You might want to protect the visiting child. You might even feel inclined to compensate in some way on behalf of your child's guest. Before you decide that your child is a monster, consider his agenda and how it differs from yours.

Some children are possessive of their environment. Initially, they may not want to share. Some become anxious when a friend visits. If a friend acts as if your child's toys belong to him, this could really be a problem. Your child does not understand why you want him to be especially nice when he feels threatened.

As a parent, you value sharing, politeness, understanding, graciousness, and other social niceties. Your child may be furious that this dumb visitor is getting special attention from his own mother! He is in no frame of mind to share everything and behave marvelously. He knows he doesn't have to be this good when he's alone. By overburdening your child with expectations, you may be ruining his fun. He may think, "This kid wants to play with all my special toys, my sister (or brother) is bugging me to play with us when I want to have my friend to myself, and my mother is giving me a bad time!" What starts out to be fun ends in misery for all concerned. Once again, clarification is in order.

First Step

Set guidelines ahead of time. Tell your child that if he wants his friend to visit, he'll have to understand the rules. He should think beforehand which toys he wants to share with his friend and which toys he wants to keep especially for himself. The special toys he will put away before his friend arrives. You should be empathetic and say that you understand that it's his right to do this. If he says to you, "I don't want to share any of them!" you should let him know that he'll have to pick some toys that can be shared if he expects to have a visitor.

Your child might feel relieved after you establish this structure, because he will feel that you are protecting his right to his toys. He will also feel that he has control over choosing which of his toys he wants to share. This will also stop the arguing between you and your child.

Second Step

When you've established the preceding guidelines, you can tell your child that rules will also be made for his brother or sister. Tell him that most of the time he'll be able to play with his friend if he wants to, but if his brother or sister doesn't have a visitor, then a few games will have to be shared. As a parent, you will protect your child's right to be alone with his friend most of the time, if he chooses. You will tell his sister or brother that it is *his* guest. They will have the same opportunity to play alone with *their* friend the next time they have a visitor.

Children under six years old will have a difficult time understanding why they can't play with their older brother or sister the entire time. In this case, it is important to try and make arrangements for the younger child by giving him something special to do, such as spending playtime with you. However, each sibling must realize that there are times when he will not be included in the other's activities.

Third Step

If your child fights with his friends, use the techniques I have mentioned in the sibling section. Come into the room and say to your child and his friends, "Let's all play this game together." Now, you may want to say to me, "You're crazy, with all the other things I have to do!" For a child whose behavior with visitors needs improvement, ten minutes of parental intervention can be helpful. The idea is to give him positive encouragement to settle disagreements without fighting.

Fourth Step

Occasionally your child will be argumentative even after the preceding techniques have been applied. Send him to his room—even though his visitor is present. Tell him to think about playing without arguing. If he continues to argue, his friend will have to go home early. He will be embarrassed. He will also learn that embarrassment is a consequence of inappropriate behavior. You are not telling your child he's a no-good, worthless person. You are telling him he'll have to change his behavior.

You must alert the parents involved if you anticipate a problem. They might have to pick up their child early. Be observant. Become aware before you get locked in. Simply let the friend know that he hasn't done anything wrong (if he hasn't), but that you have to teach your child how to behave with visitors.

If the friend's behavior has been inappropriate, you must negotiate something with his parents. Tell them their child is having a hard time playing, and you have to send him home early. Some parents may be offended. If you tell them you'd like to work it out, they are likely to cooperate. Some children may be embarrassed and resentful. They must learn that their inappropriate behavior will require consequences and you are going to take the time to teach them to improve their behavior.

6

Other Issues in the Home

PRIVACY

You are entitled to privacy from your child. This means privacy in your room and in the bathroom—and time to make love in peace.

Your child is also entitled to solitary time according to her individual needs. She is entitled to talk on the phone without your eavesdropping, and her room should be immune to search and seizure.

You must let your child know what your expectations are about privacy. Make fair but simple rules for her to follow. Normally, she is going to see you in your bedroom or bathroom from time to time. There shouldn't be a huge mystery about these rooms. As an adult, you need not explain your requirements of privacy to your child. Regardless of how curious your child is, she must realize that you expect her cooperation.

First Step

Outline to your child that there are occasions when Mom and Dad need time to themselves. Establish rules. When you are in the bedroom, she should knock. If you say you want to be alone, she should respect that.

A very young child will have difficulty with this. Nonetheless, the sooner you begin, the better. You must begin to apply consequences for failure to respect your privacy. Remember, you know which consequences are important to your child.

Second Step

Provide your child with a structure when you will need private time. For example, the sooner you let her know ahead of time, the easier it will be for her to stick to your schedule. If you prepare her by saying Dad needs private time for a half hour when he comes home from work, your child is more likely to give him that half hour. She is reassured that she will be with her father when the time is up.

If you want your child to learn to respect your need for privacy, you should tell her that she can also have her time for privacy if she wants it. If you respect her needs, she will be more likely to respect yours. There is nothing wrong with a closed door. Do not say, "We'll be out in a few minutes!" and then emerge forty-five minutes later. Your child will not believe you the next time you say, "In a few minutes." Many parents don't keep track of the time, and they make promises that are unfair to their children. It's very important that you be specific about the time. As you become more aware of what you're doing, you will do this automatically.

SEXUAL BEHAVIOR

Parents say, "What should I do when I find my kid in the room playing doctor with his friend?" or "Good grief, my child was holding his penis right in front of my girlfriend!" or "My little girl is always putting her hand between her legs" or "My child wants to come in the bathroom with me all the time, and I swear he's looking at me in a real funny way" or "I found my boy reading Playboy. What do I do? My darn husband always forgets and leaves it laying around" or "My little boy is beginning to hug me in a way that makes me feel uncomfortable."

Since children have sexual feelings, and at an early age, it is important to deal with these feelings even when it makes parents uncomfortable to do so.

No one ever warns prospective parents that their children are apt to openly express their sexual feelings in silly and inappropriate ways. However, very early in life children show an interest in these feelings by expressing curiosity about their bodies and those of the adults to whom they feel close. The myth persists that children do not think about these things very much and if it appears that they do, the situation is rarely taken seriously by their parents.

Sexual exploration is an important part of your child's growth. Your child's agenda is to understand that he or she is a sexual being and that parents are sexual beings. Children want to know the meaning of these interesting and wonderful feelings that are developing. If your little boy asks, "Why is your penis so big?" or if your little girl asks, "Why don't I have a penis, Daddy?" you look at your spouse in disbelief. You would probably try to divert your child by saying, "Would you like your breakfast now?" Perhaps you would laugh out loud and remark, "You're too young to understand" or "Don't ask such silly things." You wonder what in the world you are going to say to your child.

You may be a liberated parent who gives a detailed thesis on sexuality in response to any sexually oriented question. Or, because you were not helped to cope with your own sexuality, you probably want to avoid the issue, yet you'd like your child to be more comfortable with her sexuality than you were.

Your child's agenda is appropriate curiosity, interest in new feelings, and a general awareness of herself and those closest to her in a physical and sexual sense. Usually, your child is not asking for a lecture on sexuality. She is not interested in an extended explanation, she simply wants to understand in her own terms. For example, when she asks, "Why do you have a peepee?" she is expressing a need to understand or to be interested in this part of your body. A simple comment would be, "I see you're interested in talking to me about my penis, which is what men and boys have." Most of the time, your child will walk away, delighted and satisfied. The confusion comes when you feel or act uncomfortable, which she will notice, causing her to become even more curious. Because of your obvious discomfort or apparent anxiety, she will think that she has said or done something wrong.

First Step

Take your cue from your little girl. If she asks questions like, "Why don't I have a penis?" you should say, "Little girls have vaginas and little boys have penises." Then wait and see if she asks you more. If she says, "But I want one!" say, "I think you're telling me this because you want to be like your dad because you love him so much, but girls and moms have vaginas. That's part of being a girl, and having a penis is part of being a boy."

In this way, you are simply responding to the comfort you feel with your own gender and helping your child feel the same. You don't have to worry excessively that this kid has the famous "penis envy" problem and really wants to be a man or that she has some deep-seated problem. Most likely your child will soon get bored and walk away because you have answered her sufficiently. In this area, being a good observer of your attitude and your tone is extremely important. You can give her a feeling that questions of a sexual nature are too uncomfortable for you to discuss. This could make your child overly anxious or overly curious.

Second Step

Express feelings about sexual matters openly. For example, let's say you find your child playing doctor with a sibling or a friend. Do not walk into her room and say, "What the heck are you doing? Get dressed right now and stop all that nonsense!" Do not say to the visiting child, "You have to go right home and maybe Jane can see you next year!" Do say to your child as you walk in the room, "I can see that you kids wanted to know what it is like to play without your clothes on and touch each other to see what it feels like. Now that you have done that, I think it's time for you to get dressed and do something different. It is my rule that this is not an acceptable way to play." If she says, "Why? We didn't do anything wrong!" you say, "I want you to know that I don't think you did anything bad, but your bodies belong to you, and it is my rule that you don't touch each other like that any more. If you can't play appropriately, I will have to limit your time together. I hope you can control yourselves so I don't have to do that." You can use this type of dialogue for many kinds of situations involving exploratory sexual behavior. Acknowledging your child's curiosity, showing her that this is something that can be discussed, and then setting appropriate limits with appropriate consequences is a routine you may adopt for sexual issues.

Again, if your attitude is matter-of-fact and you are still concerned, your child will not feel guilty or bad for what she has done. One of the hardest things to do is to remain calm when you find that your child is involved in unacceptable behavior.

Third Step

Do not feel that you have to answer every question. For example, you may find your child holding his penis after you've told him he's done that long enough. Then he says, "Why can't I?" Don't get into a long dissertation about how it will fall off, how terrible it will look if people see him, or that he'll grow up to be a pervert. This is one of those questions that simply does not deserve an explanation because all he's really telling you is that he just wants to keep holding himself.

You might be confused because you are dealing with *sex*. Just say, "I want you to stop because this is one of my rules. If you can't stop playing that way, you will have to go to bed early." Treat your child's sexual behavior as you would any other. Give a consequence if he doesn't follow the rules. If you follow through matter-of-factly, he will generally not persist. In other words, if your agenda is confused, you will make the sexual issue much more involved than it needs to be. Your child's agenda involves a sexual curiosity. He's simply trying to figure out what it's all about. Normally, it goes no further than that.

Fourth Step

This step is for parents who have trouble controlling their anger. If you come into the room with fire in your eyes, you are likely to convey to your child that she has just committed the sexual crime of the century. If you're not prepared for her sex play, you might understandably overreact. Once you've observed that you are overreacting, go back into her room and say, "I got too mad about what you were doing, and I just want you to know that I shouldn't have gotten so upset. You didn't do anything terrible, but there is a rule about that kind of play." As we discussed in the second and third steps, you might say, "You kids can't play that way, you've seen each other nude and from now on the rule is that you must play with your clothes on. If you can't follow this rule, there will be no playing in the room alone."

Fifth Step

If your child's sexual behavior seems to persist, try not to worry. Tell her that anytime she wants to discuss the difference between boys and girls, look at some books, or ask questions, you will be glad to talk to her.

Sixth Step

Remember that if your child's sexual curiosity continues to persist with behavior such as looking at *Playboy* magazine or touching you in a way that suggests sexual overtones, this is a normal phase of his sexual feelings and curiosity. Say, "I know you like to read *Playboy* and I guess you are real interested in what women look like in the nude, but I think you have seen enough of the magazine so I am going to put it away. When you need to, you can come to me, and we will find books that can help you understand about the difference between men and women."

A parent who is not comfortable with the "liberal" approach may say, "I think you have seen enough of those pictures, and I don't want you to keep looking at them. If you can't follow my rule, you will have to miss your favorite program" (or use another appropriate consequence for your child). Being aware means you must remain calm. If you stop your child, you aren't damaging his curiosity or sexuality. He will eventually move out of this stage because his curiosity has been dealt with honestly and appropriately. He will not be overly preoccupied with sex.

On the other hand, if you habitually overreact, your child is likely to become overly concerned about his sexuality. Appropriate permission to deal with his feelings will allow him to view sex as a natural function rather than a mystery or something bad.

You will notice that I didn't devote a great deal of time to locked-in struggles. If you get locked into a battle regarding your child's sexual behavior, I strongly recommend professional help.

MASTURBATION

Most parents worry about masturbation. Masturbation is a normal phase in the development of sexuality. However, you may have difficulty accepting this, particularly if your child has masturbated openly or has embarrassed you.

Children masturbate because of the need for self-gratification and sometimes because of anxiety. When you initially see your child masturbating, you might start fantasizing, "Oh good grief, what if she does this in front of my mother? My kid will be a sex pervert by the time she's twelve years old. What will the neighbors think?" One of the famous tricks is for a parent to try to grab a child's hands from between her legs in a tug-of-war effort to keep the kid from playing with herself.

First Step

Acknowledge to your child that you see that he or she likes to touch his penis or her vagina. This should be handled as any behavior that is considered unacceptable. In some cases it is that simple. If you are understanding and your expectations are reasonable, you will not become inappropriately worried about his or her behavior.

Or, you might tell your child, "If you feel the need to touch yourself, I want you to do it in your room and not while watching TV or in front of us." By stating it simply, you are not judging your child, and you are telling her that you're not interested in watching her do that.

You will begin to help her see without the need for an explanation, that this is a private act. If your child insists on knowing why, tell her it's just one of your rules. Unless this is a particularly troubled area for her because she is relieving a great deal of anxiety, these techniques will have some effect on her behavior. Usually young children masturbate, but sporadically. A locked-in struggle over masturbation indicates a need for professional help.

PART III
BEHAVIOR OUTSIDE THE HOME

7

Public Behavior

MARKETS

Some of the most embarrassing moments with children occur in public places. A parent is understandably more uncomfortable in this situation because his obvious lack of parenting skills is displayed for others to see.

At the market, for example, your agenda is to buy food. In your fantasy, your child calmly follows you and reminds you of the items that you need. Perhaps he even removes a few things from the shelves for you and stands quietly in line while you check out. He never whines for the candy he's seen on television.

Your child's agenda in the market is to look at all of the interesting items on the shelves, remember everything that the television programs tried to influence him to buy, run down the aisles, and generally create chaos. He also has the idea that Mom is there to buy him lots of goodies, and it's a rude awakening when this doesn't happen.

A market is also an interesting place for your child to disappear and hide—usually when you're ready to leave—and to sneak everything he can reach into the basket. He will want to talk to people and to comment about them. "Look, Mommy, there's a fat lady!" he might say, or "Look how many wrinkles that man has!" He doesn't do this to be a brat. He is simply curious. Virtually everything about life is new to him. A child between the ages of three and six will not have the awareness to restrain comment.

Trying to act like this pesty child is not yours rarely works, nor does giving him that quiet, irritated reaction, "Just a moment, can't you see I'm busy?" It's easy to become self-conscious, to think everyone in the line is looking at you. You imagine everyone is judging you and your child. A major anxiety provoker!

When your child's behavior in the market is persistently difficult, you will need to use some unaccustomed methods. You must set your priorities. If you take him to the market and he misbehaves, your priority is to teach him how to behave in the market. Your priority is not to stock up on food. You may say to yourself, "Not go there to buy food? Isn't that what a market is for? Do I have to starve for a month just to teach my kid how to behave in a supermarket?" No, you don't have to starve. You do have to establish procedures.

First Step

Tell your child what the rules are ahead of time. He must stay with you and do what you tell him. He's not to hide behind the dairy containers or jump into other people's food baskets. He may talk to people, but when you tell him to stop what he's doing, he must do so. He may ask for one item. You should define in advance what kinds of items are permissible. If you're conscious of nutrition, allow him to have some sugarless gum or something similar that will be agreeable to him.

Second Step

Tell him that even if you're standing in line with all of your groceries, if he can't control himself you will put the basket aside, take him outside, and make him sit in the car for five minutes. (You should stand outside of the car, looking away from him in order not to give him any attention.) After five minutes, allow him to enter the market again to see if his behavior is acceptable. This is his last try; if this does not work, he will have to go home and face a consequence.

Third Step

If you try a second time and he persists in being uncooperative, you must be willing to leave the food (not a very popular tactic with grocery managers, incidentally!), go home, and give him an immediate consequence. This experience will help him learn that you are able to control his behavior in public situations.

Fourth Step

Prepare him to try again the next time you go to the market. Tell him you know he can do it, and ask him if he wants to try again. If he doesn't come through, you simply say to him, "I guess you weren't ready," and then take him home and gradually increase the consequence.

An alternate step is for two adults to shop together. This will allow one of them to continue getting the food while the other one can take the child out to the car if it's necessary. Again, your child must sit in the back seat while you or your spouse stand outside of the car or sit in the front seat reading a magazine or a book. Do not attract his attention because it will affect his behavior. He must feel the impact of what he has done.

If you are a single parent and this behavior has become extreme, another alternative is to have a friend (a very good friend!) available. That way you can take your child to your friend's house, leave him, and go back to the store. You must make everyone at your friend's house understand it is not playtime for him and that the adult shouldn't make the time fun while you're gone. Thus, he experiences that there's going to be consistency even with friends or relatives.

If you're unwilling to practice these techniques, don't expect your child to behave better just because you tell him to. Teaching him appropriate behavior is your primary concern. He must know that. Any time you fail to follow through on a consequence, you've lost your credibility.

You may find it necessary to disrupt your normal way of doing things. However, in order to teach your child that you can deal with his behavior under any circumstance, you must sometimes take unusual steps. If you can accept the initial inconvenience, you may actually begin to like your child.

The preceding techniques are applicable for all types of public behavior. Particularize them for your situation, as you continue to observe what works for you and your child.

RESTAURANT BEHAVIOR

Once in a while when you're in a restaurant you may see someone else's children eating calmly and quietly for well over half an hour. You'll probably check every now and then, certain that any moment they'll become rowdy and noisy (like your own), but you can't believe your eyes! You may say to your kid, "Now why can't you be like them?" What you don't know is that the entire family is on one hundred milligrams of Stelazine and they probably aren't doing any better with their children than you are. They just decided to take the easy way out.

When eating out, the parent's agenda is to enjoy stimulating adult conversation and to introduce the child to good food. You are, essentially, asking your child to sit for a long time without becoming impatient or disruptive.

Your child's agenda includes eating as quickly as possible or not at all. The chances of the latter occurring increases as the restaurant becomes more expensive! He is more interested in what is happening at everyone else's table. He wants to play as many interesting games as the table setting allows.

For young children, sitting still in a restaurant is torture. Sliding under the table is much more fun. Just imagine! He might find old gum, pennies, even food that he prefers. Scooting under the table is like deep sea diving without the water, and it's a lot more fun than sitting and listening to adults talking.

First Step

Become realistic about your expectations. Make an estimate on how long you can expect appropriate behavior from your child in a restaurant. If you get twenty minutes from a three- to six-year-old, you are doing well. It's not fair to expect a very young child to sit quietly and listen to adults talk. Older children should be able to sit approximately half an hour. Obviously, fast food places are the easiest way to take children out to eat.

It's not realistic to take children to restaurants that take half an hour just to serve. Your child may not be ready for this experience. What feels special to you—beautiful decor, a waiter in a tux, your own dressy clothes—may create tension for your child. A six-year-old doesn't care about the waiter's French accent. He thinks, "Who cares? I'd rather go to McDonald's." No wonder he won't eat! I'm trying to make the agenda point—again. Fancy restaurants and young children just don't work.

Second Step

If you must take your young child to a good restaurant, tell him in a very caring way, "I know that sometimes you have trouble sitting in a restaurant, but Mommy and Daddy would like to take you out to eat with us. We'd like you to try not to run around, get up, or make lots of noise. We'll let you bring one of your favorite things to draw with, but if you have trouble controlling yourself, we will be forced to take you out to the car, and you will have to wait until you can control yourself."

Third Step

If you have taken your child out to the car and he says he is ready to try again, but once inside the restaurant he starts misbehaving, you must tell him, "I'm going to tell you one more time to get control of yourself or we're going home and you're going right to bed." If you show him that his behavior is more important than finishing your meal, if you're willing to teach him that his appropriate behavior is your number one priority, he will learn.

If you show your child that you're upset about leaving the restaurant and shout things like, "Now see what you've done. I didn't get to finish my $9.95 lamb chops!" he will sense that it's worse on you than it is on him. Sometimes you will really have to fake it, even though you are salivating for that lamb chop. Also, if you overdo acting upset, you might make your child feel overly guilty.

Some parents might be thinking, "Well, gosh, my child is making me leave the restaurant and I don't get to finish my food. Isn't he winning?" Your child is not thinking in terms of "winning." The key issue is establishing the priority of teaching him acceptable restaurant behavior.

Go to a restaurant close to your home so that one parent can take the child home if necessary. When you take him home, you must give a consequence. If you don't follow through, he will learn that you do not intend to deal with his inappropriate behavior.

I have used the extreme example of a special restaurant only to emphasize that even if the situation is an uncommon occurrence, it is important to follow through. You must be systematic. Deprive yourself of a nice evening if you must, to show your child that his behavior is the most important thing to you. And you may have to interrupt only two or three meals in order to teach him to behave in restaurants. If your techniques are weak, you're destined for many half-eaten lamb chops!

Being a good observer means becoming aware of your child's readiness to behave appropriately in restaurants. It's unrealistic to expect him to behave when he has previously demonstrated by his actions that he is incapable of handling the situation.

DOCTORS AND DENTISTS

Adults and children have similar agendas regarding doctors and dentists. Your child picks up messages from you that it isn't fun going to the dentist or doctor. You might not realize it, but he is probably listening when you say something like. "Darn it, my tooth hurts and I guess I have to visit that darn dentist," and, "Gee, I haven't had a checkup in ages, but I just dread going to the doctor." What your child picks up is that the doctor or dentist's office is not a place of joy but one of anxiety and suffering.

If you don't give your child an idea of what to expect, he might feel as if he has been tricked by you. You tell him that the nice doctor is just going to examine him, and without warning the next thing he knows, a strange tube is being shoved inside his body. In stark terror he lets out a wail that is heard ten floors below, and the doctor asks you why your child is so upset.

You might be the type of parent who doesn't tell your child where or when you're taking him. Suddenly he finds himself in the waiting room of a horrible place, and visions of his last nightmarish visit come back to him. Your child runs for the door, anxious to avoid the man who told him to open his mouth and then went to work with a buzz saw. This probably sounds like an exaggeration, but when your child is anxious, he will fantasize and make my description seem mild.

One reason you try not to let your child know that he's going to the doctor or dentist is because this is an experience that we know may be truly painful. It gives adults a great deal of anxiety, and they wish there were some way to help their children avoid this discomfort. You feel helpless because you are unable to prevent your child's experience no matter how much it hurts. The main reason you may avoid this issue is that you are afraid that if you are unable to assure him that the examination will be painless, he won't be able to handle the truth about the experience. If a child is under six years of age you might be worried that he will not understand your explanation about going to the doctor. It is my opinion that there are definitely ways to explain this issue to your child, and I hope the following examples will be helpful. After that age, he generally knows what you're talking about, and it's hard to avoid the subject since he will probably ask direct, specific questions.

First Step

Prepare your child a week in advance. Remind him once or twice that he's going to the doctor. Avoiding the issue only increases many children's fears because it doesn't give them a chance to grapple with the real fear of visiting the doctor or dentist.

Second Step

Stop conning your child. Do not say, "It's not going to hurt," or, "The doctor only wants to talk to you." Call the doctor. Find out what the examination will entail. If, for example, the doctor tells you that the procedure will be lengthy and painful, don't lie to your child. Say, "Yes, it is going to hurt and it will last a while, but I will be right there with you. This has to be done even though I know it's hard. It will help you get better." After you've explained the technique to your child, let him know that if he needs to talk to you about it again, he can come to you before the appointment with the doctor.

If your child is under six years old, you might want to dramatize the procedure by playacting. Get a toy Doctor Kit with make-believe items like a hypodermic needle and a stethoscope. Have your child try them on you,. Talk about what hurts and what doesn't. If you know that he is going to have a shot, you should take the needle and say, "When you go to the doctor, he will do this to you." Take the play hypodermic needle and put it up to your child's arm and say, "See, it only hurts a little and only for a minute." If he acts fearful, have him try the needle on you first to give him a feeling of control. Use all of the items in the kit to give him a feeling of what an examination is like. Do this in a fun way.

Overcome any reservations you may have about feeling silly. The sense of control your child experiences will calm his fears.

Also, the more you monitor your own anxieties, the more effective your communication will be with your child.

Third Step

Be aware of your own behavior when you tell your child that the procedure might be lengthy or painful. If you are upset by his complaints, you will only increase his anxiety. Your difficult task is to show him that you can handle his worry, anxiety, and pain. For example, say to your child, "I know this is hard but sometimes we have to do the things we don't like. I know that you're going to feel better when it's all over."

Since you're not a robot, it is normal to show that you worry. If you do this, say to your child, "Sometimes you may see me acting worried. It is because I love you a lot and I don't like to see you in pain. I really know, though, that we can work this problem out together." You are basically making him aware of his feelings while acknowledging yours and supporting a very realistic struggle that isn't easy for anybody.

Fourth Step

This step is necessary if you've been locked in with anxiety and worry. When your child is extremely agitated by a visit to the doctor, you must be assertive with the doctor. Tell him politely that your child is upset. Ask the doctor to take some time to demonstrate his technique, explain what he's going to do, and above all, reassure your child.

If your child exhibits unusual difficulties, it is important to seek a doctor who is sensitive. I've counseled many adults who had disturbing childhood experiences with the doctor, and they are still afraid of doctors and hospitals.

Some situations require professional help. If your child does not respond to your changed behavior, his fears may be too deeply rooted and complex. By all means seek professional help. You don't want him to grow up chronically avoiding medical and/or dental help when it is necessary.

8

Car Behavior

Many parents dread going anywhere with their children because they think a car is a place to do acrobatics or punch out a brother or sister. Knowing that your hands are on the wheel and you are not an octopus, they are in a position to do once-in-a-lifetime stunts. This is one of those frustrating times when Mom or Dad can't have eyes, ears, and hands in three places at once.

Your child learns that it's hard for you to attend to her behavior while you're driving. Since your attention is on the road, you are reduced to retaliating with threats. Yet statements like, "You're going to make me crash," or "Do you want to get us all killed?" will make your child even more anxious because she anticipates the impending doom about to befall the family. This does not improve her behavior.

Do not say, "You are making me a nervous wreck," or threaten her with, "You are going to get it!" Such statements communicate your feeling of powerlessness.

First, I will talk about how to handle one child; then I'll discuss how to handle more than one child in a car. If you are only taking one child in a car, the problem is not quite as complicated. Kids tend to be less of a problem in a car when siblings are not around.

First Step

Set clear guidelines. As usual, try not to scream or yell. In a non-threatening but firm way, tell your child that there are going to be some new rules and she will have to control her behavior.

Second Step

Explain that if she can't sit quietly (in the front seat) without making too much noise or bouncing up and down, she will have to sit in the back. Assure her that you would really like her to sit up front, that you want to be with her, but she must control herself. You are conveying a sense of concern as well as a clear set of rules.

Third Step

Do not yell, even if the behavior persists. Simply tell your child that you will give her two minutes to regain control. If she can't do this, tell her when she gets home there will be a consequence. Be specific; the next time she does it, the consequence will be longer.

Fourth Step

If you're taking your child to an event she's looking forward to—a movie or a party—tell her that you will take her home if she doesn't regain control. Give her one chance. Once you've turned the car around, ask her if she's ready to try one more time. If she can regain control, give her the chance and continue on to the party or movie.

If she can't regain control, even if she begs, cries, or whines, take her home as a consequence for not listening.

If your child's poor car behavior has been persistent, you must be systematic. If you are meeting other people at the movie or a party, say to them that you're working on a problem and your plans might be interrupted. If you don't have this understanding in advance, you will be uncomfortable, and less likely to follow through.

Fifth Step

If you *must* go somewhere, you obviously can't turn around and go home. In this case, let your child know that if she doesn't control herself there will be a consequence when she gets home. The consequence will be increased each time she's out of control.

Now we will discuss the steps that deal with more than one child in a car.

First Step

You assign the seating. If the children argue, you will assign seat rotation. You will not argue with your children concerning how they feel about it. You will not keep charts of seat rotation. Your only concern is that your children regain control of their behavior.

Second Step

Unfortunately, separating the kids doesn't always stop the arguing. Even after you have put one child in the front and one in the back, they may tease or taunt one another. If they continue this disruptive behavior, let them know that if they can't control themselves, you will pull off the road. Then you should stop the car until they listen to you. Now, you might be saying, "This man doesn't live in the real world. What if I have an appointment or I have to get someplace?"

If behavior in the car is an important issue, you must make that issue your number one priority for awhile. So, once you've pulled off the road and have shown them that you will wait for five minutes, try a second time. If they are still out of control, stop again and wait longer. This is particularly effective if you are going somewhere that they want to visit. It does not work as well in the case of an "unpleasant" experience like visiting the doctor, the dentist, or a relative they don't care about.

When the issue is your appointment, let them know that you will enforce a consequence when you return home.

Third Step

Occasionally you will be in such a hurry that you cannot stop or turn around and go home. It is crucial for you to tell the children that even though you don't have time to stop and deal with their behavior, there will be consequences. If you follow through, the behavior should improve.

If your child makes you turn around when going to a movie you wanted to see or to a party that you wanted to attend, don't think she is winning. Once again, you are teaching her that your priority is her behavior. Her behavior is even more important than your convenience or pleasure. When your child understands that you will give up your own enjoyment to help her learn appropriateness, the seriousness of the issue becomes clear.

CAR POOLING

Most parents have had firsthand experience with hauling children around. The daily routine of car pooling does include certain elements of danger. A typical day might begin with you as the driver begging your child to get into the car while she screams, "No, I won't!" The next child, feeling just as rebellious, promptly kicks her fellow passenger in the knee after which the next passenger punches someone in the tummy. Another child might have a hard time separating from his parent and will bawl his lungs out. The result is that you have four upset, fighting kids to cope with. The mothers of these little darlings (who are lucky enough not to be driving that day!) simply say, "Bye, Honey, I'll see you later." Again, you, the driving parent, are left not only with the task of getting the children to school on time, but also with trying to be a psychologist to all of them.

There are other frustrating aspects of car pooling. There is the mother-driver who rolls up with five kids in her big Lincoln Continental and honks the horn impatiently even though she sees through the window that your child is still at the breakfast table. Mrs. Lincoln Continental has a number of options: she can wait calmly, send hideous looks toward the house, or gun the motor nineteen times as loudly as possible. If nothing else, the latter makes all the kids in the car nervous. If she's lucky, it will also evoke enough guilt so that you and your child will get up earlier the next morning.

Another favorite technique of the mother who is made to wait is heavy sighing, usually accompanied with comments like, "Well kids, I guess you're going to be late." To really instill guilt, she might add, "Well, I guess you're going to miss the special game

Mrs. Harmon arranged for all of you today." These are very indirect and ineffective ways of telling the offending mother that it is inconvenient to be kept waiting. The victims of this technique are the children.

What are the agendas in car pooling? Your agenda is to pick up all of the kids on time, have them all walk to the car calmly waving good-bye to their parents (with big smiles, of course), and have them sit in any seat that's available without complaint. You want to drive happily off to school while they make interesting conversation.

The child's agenda for car pooling, as you might have suspected, is quite different. Sometimes she is not in the mood to go to school, so she is irritable to begin with. A young child might not want to leave her parent. If she's older, she may not be interested in going to school. Her major concern is that she not sit next to dumb Mary Jane or smelly Billy. It is helpful to think about what it means to a child to be in a car pool.

One problem is space. Children must sit close together. There aren't enough windows to go around. They have no toys, and there's nothing to do but look straight ahead. I'm not suggesting that you take all the seats out of your car and install a playroom, but you must understand why the car pool is such a strain for your child.

First Step

Adults should cooperate in establishing guidelines for car pooling, taking into account what is comfortable for the parents. Parents should meet periodically to discuss the car pool. A little time spent discussing problems could reduce stress for both parents and children. How car pooling is handled affects the way a child gets started in school that day. It can set either a very comfortable tone or a very difficult one. Discuss misbehavior and the other issues that arise. Have an agreement in advance about how the driver-parent will handle these issues.

Second Step

Discuss what to do if a parent is late. You may decide, for example, that the late parent will be responsible for getting his child to school if the driver-parent has been kept past a prescribed time.

Third Step

Parents should agree on guidelines for handling behavior; they need to agree about what are the most important issues. Calming the child, if she is upset, should be your priority. Helping a child with her emotions is more important than an occasional tardiness. Remember, you have established this in advance with the other parents. You should support each other against the child's potential manipulations.

Say to the other children, "Jane is upset, and her mom needs to help her calm down before we go to school." Even if Jane has to go back into the house for a few minutes, this teaches the child that adults are concerned about her emotional well-being and that getting to school on time is secondary.

Fourth Step

Beyond six years of age, children are sometimes just angry and irritable. They will act pouty and unhappy for seemingly no reason. By this age the child might feel social disapproval, and she will cry hysterically just because she doesn't want to go to school. Again, the preceding steps apply. The driving parent can be very helpful by explaining to the children that the child who is upset is struggling, and that they must try to understand. This doesn't mean lecturing them or getting mad. It means saying something like, "It seems that Jane has a hard time getting started in the morning, and I hope that all of you kids will try to be understanding and make her feel comfortable even if Jane is upset." Now, unless some of the kids are just looking for trouble—which isn't typical of most kids—this could help. With appropriate and sensitive adult assistance, many children are willing to understand other kids' struggles.

Like most of the other issues discussed, you must focus your attention on the importance of a child's emotional needs rather than on the need to arrive at school on time. In car pooling, the basic issue is your impact on your own child. However, you must also deal with the other parents and their children.

LONGER TRIPS IN THE CAR

Parental fantasies about trips in the car tend to be unrealistic. You are looking forward to some rest and relaxation, you want to get away from tension, and you hope that your child will experience something exciting and educational. If you are a true optimist, you envision enjoying your spouse and rekindling some romantic feelings for each other.

For practical reasons, you can't apply the suggestions for in-town trips to vacations. It's not easy to turn around and go home when you're on a four-hundred-mile trip from Los Angeles to San Francisco. When your child cries out in the middle of nowhere, "I've gotta go to the bathroom, now!" you can't drop her off at some strange motel or leave her at the Greyhound Bus Depot to return home. What do you do?

Let's look at your child's agenda. You may have raised her expectations to interest her in the trip. You might have told her that she's going to have a "grand old time" during the drive, watching all of the wonderful sights from the car window. What your child expects from this is a Disneyland experience with everything focused on her pleasure.

You haven't told her that sometimes you'll be in the middle of nowhere, that she'll have to wait to go to the bathroom, wait to get something to eat, and wait to get some rest. When you reach an unpopulated stretch of highway and your kid yells out, "Mommy, Daddy, I'm hungry!", all she hears from you is a gruff, "In a while ... you'll just have to wait," or "I have one candy bar left and that's it." Where is the amusement park experience for which she yearns? All she's seen are gas stations, coffee shops, the side of the road, and an occasional cow standing in a field doing what comes naturally.

When your child realizes that these inconveniences are the "interesting things'' you meant, she becomes restless. All she wants to know at that point is how long it is going to be before you arrive at your destination.

Being cramped together in a car for a long time when everyone's defenses are down and reality sets in can be a frustrating, exhausting, and unpleasant experience. You must plan for it!

Some parents are able to start traveling with their children when they are very young. This has given them time to become acclimated to the difficulties of traveling with children. If you are not one of the lucky ones, the following will help.

First Step

Start, if possible, by taking your child on short trips. A two- or three-year-old can usually manage a hundred miles to a grandparent's house. Test her ability to deal with the car trip. Take other types of trips—again in order to see how she adjusts to the experience.

Realistically, many children between three and five years of age are just not ready for long trips. For example, a very impatient child would find it exceedingly difficult to sit for long periods of time. It isn't fair to blame your child for this difficulty. If she has trouble sitting still at home or at school, you can imagine what confinement in a car will feel like to her.

Even some children who are older than five may still not be ready for long trips. It isn't worth it to try to fulfill your fantasy of a wonderful family outing when you will probably return totally exhausted. Sometimes you must be realistic about your child's ability to adapt.

Second Step

Structure your trip according to your child's age and interest. Take along some toys, games, and projects—plan activities that will be a diversion for her. Plan systematic times to stop. Instead of saying, "If we can just keep going, we will make Evansville by 2:00 and stay right on our schedule!" take the time to get out and stretch. If your child can count on times when she can get out of the car and go to the bathroom or just play around, you should see some improvement in her behavior. Even taking an extra hour or two to reach your destination is worth the difference if the trip is made pleasurable.

Third Step

Even with the structured, systematic stops, your child may become unruly. Much of this behavior comes from stress. If your child persists, you must say something like, "I know this is difficult, but I want you to control yourself." If she continues this behavior, you should tell her that she won't be able to do some of the things that you had told her she'd be doing on the trip.

For example, at each stop along the way, she might have been promised a small souvenir or her favorite candy—her reward for behaving. If she doesn't behave, there shouldn't be a major punishment because a trip can cause regressive behavior in your child. Taking away the candy or souvenir she had looked forward to is sufficient. With a reward system for good behavior, you are able to remind her that if she controls herself, there is something positive in it for her.

It is quite possible that some of this won't work. But it isn't realistic to expect your child to behave well on long trips. It is your job as a parent, however, to control your own feelings and to keep in mind the differences in agendas that I have outlined. In other words, if you're not realistic about these suggestions, it's your responsibility to control yourself, if you can, and to understand that sometimes you're expecting too much from your child.

9

Neighborhood Children

Sometimes you might catch yourself very casually peeking out of the window from behind the curtains or shutters, trying to get a glimpse of what's going on outside. Often a blood-curdling scream disrupts what you're doing. Many times your child bursts through the door, complaining, "Johnny and Jerry won't let me play with them" or "Jerry hit me on the head with a baseball bat."

Depending on what kind of parent you are, your comment might be, "Uh huh," which ends the conversation or, if you're an investigative type, "How did it happen? . . . Why do they keep picking on you? . . . Are you sure you didn't do something to cause this? . . . Why do you play with those horrible kids?"

If you're overprotective, you will launch yourself out of the door screaming at the top of your lungs, "Leave my little Tommy alone!" The kids, of course, look at you like you're completely mad. Naturally at that moment all of your neighbors come out to pick up their newspapers, get an eyeful of this maniacal parent, and agree with the kids.

Why, you ask, does this occur? Well, let's go back to the subject of agendas. You, as a parent, want your child to be the neighborhood favorite who will get along well with everyone. You want him to form deep and lasting friendships in the neighborhood, and you also want him to be able to stick up for himself.

Your child's agenda is to go out and make friends, learn about the give and take of playing with other children, and let out his frustrations. However, when he comes home, his agenda is different. You should feel fortunate if he comes home telling you he had a marvelous time because a child does not often do this. Instead, you are the person your child wants to talk to when everything goes wrong. His fantasy is that you can make everything better and that you are a safe and supportive person to whom he can tell all his troubles. He is partially right. Even though you can't magically solve his problems, you can potentially be very helpful and understanding. It isn't much different when adults come home and complain about the lousy things that happened to them at work. Your child's gory descriptions tend to make you more anxious because he has a gift for making it sound as if he's being picked on every minute.

The worst way to handle this problem is to run outside and scream and yell at the other children to leave your little Tommy alone. By doing this, you make them madder at him, since he is probably getting them in trouble with you. If they're defiant children, they'll probably just laugh in your face anyway, forcing you to use every ounce of restraint in order to avoid punching them in the nose. Nothing is solved.

First Step

This applies to children between the ages of three and six. They are more likely to listen to you than those between seven and nine years of age (because they aren't afraid of authority). Show your child that you understand what he's feeling. If he keeps complaining, empathize with him before you make any decision about what to do. Tell him that you can see he's upset and you realize that he had a rough time. Ask, "What was it like when you weren't fighting? Was playing outside today worth it?" By doing this, you're helping your child look at his overall experience rather than just the upsetting segment. It is normal for him to dramatize when he is upset. If you ask him for an assessment of his afternoon, you're giving him an opportunity to make sense of the situation. He remembers that the overall experience of playing was fun. He'll probably admit that there were lots of good times between the shoving, pushing, and name calling.

Second Step

Ask your child whether or not he thinks he can handle the situation. Say, "Are you able to play with them?" This is an attempt to help him make a realistic decision.

If your child is between three and six years old, you may need to observe some of his play—particularly when he's in your yard—to see if he needs some help. If you see that the other kids are picking on him, I would suggest that you practice deep breathing until you can walk out calmly.

Third Step

Say to the other children, "I can see that Tommy upsets you kids sometimes, but I hope you can find some way to play without upsetting one another, and if you can't, I'll have to restrict the amount of playing that can be done in our yard." As you do this, you should say to the children that you really hope they can work this out between them because if they can't control themselves, you will have to limit their time together.

If they're basically good friends, they are likely to cooperate. Do avoid long lectures. Simply remind them of the agreement. If they break their agreement, they will have to stop playing, but they can try again tomorrow.

Fourth Step

If it isn't your yard, you will have to make sure that your child knows what his options are. Tell him that his job is to come home if he can't play with the other children without fighting. Most children won't want to do this. You're trying to make your child aware of ways to solve this problem by himself. He must begin to separate himself from you. He should make every effort to walk away trying to control himself, even though some children will find this difficult to do. When he decides to play again, he will have a better chance of being accepted by the other children. Also, explain that teasing is probably inevitable.

Suppose there is real trouble? Your child is really fighting with another child. Telling him to simply fight back when he's having trouble with another child is not usually a realistic suggestion. It may make him feel more pressured and, if he fails, less confident.

Fifth Step

In the event your child has been hurt, you have a number of options. It's necessary for him to feel that he will be supported while you're calling the other parent. Don't say things like, "Why did your child punch my kid in the nose?" or "Your kid is the biggest brat in the neighborhood . . . he's always causing trouble."

With the goal of reaching an understanding, say something like, "There has been a problem between your child and mine [no value judgment] and I'd like to see if we can work it out. Tommy told me that Johnny punched him, and I hope that we can have an understanding about their behavior with each other if they're going to play together in the future." You're interested in harmony, not trying to prove that the other parent is wrong.

Sixth Step

If your child has hurt another child, you may want him to apologize. A forced apology will not resolve the conflict, and it will not teach him anything.

You may say, in your child's presence, "It looks like Tommy is still too upset to apologize to you. I'm going to apologize for him right now. I think that when he's no longer mad, he will be able to talk to you about it." Your child will feel that you understand his anger, yet he will know that his appropriate behavior is still your priority.

Some children relieve their guilt by apologizing. This is not learning. To say, "I'm sorry," at the direction of a parent is to do so under duress. If you insist on your child apologizing and he will do it only because you make him, he will feel angry toward you because he is more focused on the anger than on what you're telling him to do.

An alternative to these suggestions is to tell your child, "I want you to try to apologize. I know it's hard, but if Johnny hears that you understand what you did, he might be friendlier to you. If you find that it is too hard to apologize, I'll help you." Using this approach, you will help your child understand your reason for wanting him to say, "I'm sorry"; you're supporting his struggle, and you're letting him know that you understand it isn't easy.

Both sets of parents should be supportive in identifying the areas of conflict. Make some rules for the future concerning the issues that relate to neighborhood play. When children know that the neighborhood adults are unified rather than siding with their children, behavior will improve.

PART IV
ANTISOCIAL BEHAVIOR

10

Lying

To comprehend why children sometimes do not tell the truth, you must understand a little bit about the value of fantasy in childhood. Between three and six years of age, children begin to have very rich fantasy lives. These fantasies are pleasurable to the child, and they have many levels of meaning.

Through fantasy your child is learning to use her imagination, how it feels to be angry, to have ideas about the world, and to feel a sense of power that is strong enough to combat fear. These fantasies can help control fears and anxieties; they give her the feeling that she is in control. Also, she is learning to experience great pleasure in creative thought. Sometimes this takes the form of making up stories that your child believes are true. Many times she feels that these stories are really true, and at this age such a feeling is appropriate.

As your child develops mastery of thought and verbal expression, and as she feels herself having an impact on the world, her need to fantasize decreases because she feels that she has more control of her world.

However, parents worry when their child is not truthful on every point. Once again we are back to the subject of agendas. You want reassurance that she will grow up to be an upright human being. Any indication that she might not terrifies you. Parents often think that when their child is fantasizing, she is lying in a manipulative way. A new way to think about this is to understand what you have previously talked about. A parent might say, "Boy, you have such good ideas" or "That's a wonderful story." However, if your child is actually not telling the truth, then the following section will help you.

Children don't lie! Now, you are thinking, "This guy has to be looney tunes or amoral. I thought he was on my side, and now he tells me children don't lie." Well, I am on your side. Just give me a chance to outline why children don't tell parents the truth; I'll explain the reasons that cause children to tell falsehoods.

One of the reasons is the famous "trap question." You know that your child did something; you saw her do it. Instead of saying, "I saw you take money out of the drawer," you say, "What were you doing in my room?"

"Nothing," says Jane.

"Don't tell me 'nothing,' " you say. "Did you take anything?"

"No."

"Are you sure?"

"Yes," says Jane.

She becomes more and more uncomfortable about the questioning, and she gets deeper and deeper in untruths. Backed into a corner, it becomes harder to admit things. Then you say, "I saw you take it. Why do you lie?"

You just busted her in a cops and robbers routine, questioning her and then nailing her. That's called the investigative-interrogation approach, which only increases lying! How would you like it if your boss questioned you about leaving work early? You wouldn't want to admit anything!

We think that if the kid would only admit to fibbing, then she would never do it again. But admitting things doesn't mean our behavior changes. Even if we make the issue comfortable for kids, it is not easy for them to tell the truth. Children think of themselves as either good or bad. If your child does something that she suspects you will think is wrong, she is going to feel bad. Then she'll be anxious and worry about some fantasy, which will get her into trouble. Many times when your child "lies," it is because she is worried about your reaction, and she is scared. Or, she may just want to have her own way by "lying."

What is important to your child is your attitude. If you want her to learn that lying is not a scary topic to discuss, that it's no different than other subjects, you must learn how to deal with it. Your child may feel that she's in trouble no matter what she tells you. Sometimes you tell your kid that you won't be mad. Then you find out something that is more than you anticipated. You lose control and demand, "How could you do that?" Your child concludes, "Egad. I'm really in trouble now, even though they told me everything would be OK!"

And even when your words tell your child that she won't get into trouble, often your emotional tone is noticed by her. Somehow, parents feel that if they can get their child to tell the truth, she'll never lie again. And you hope that this will lead her to feelings of remorse because she lied. Parents sometimes enjoy the fact that their child will experience feelings of remorse. They have the misconception that their child will learn from this. Sorry, folks, it doesn't work! Children don't learn through remorse. They are aware of your tone and your attitude, which causes them to feel pressure about lying. When they feel this pressure, their lying sometimes escalates. Then their feelings of discomfort increase because they don't know what to do and they are hoping that their parents will finally "get off their backs."

Sometimes you might confuse your child's fantasies and wishing with lying. For example, she might come home from school and tell you a story that she hit three home runs and was carried off the field in triumph. You may say, "Why do you make up such ridiculous stories?" or give a questioning response like, "Did you really do that?" Your child feels put down, gets angry, and says, "Yes!" Or you may say, "Why do you make things up like that if they aren't true? No one will ever believe you again . . . including me!"

Children between the ages of three and five years old and sometimes older often make up wild fantasies about monsters or develop elaborate stories about going to the store and being given candy. This is very normal at this age. You shouldn't worry because you think your child is "cracking up" when she continues coming home with wild stories about riding on a dragon's back or beating up the math teacher. Don't start interrogating your child or tell her to stop making up these tales.

Let's look at this issue. First, let's review your child's agenda. She makes things up for wish fulfillment, to make herself feel more important, to manipulate in order to get her way, and to deal with fearful situations. Your agenda is to raise a modern-day George Washington who will not tell a lie!

First Step

Let's say your child repeatedly comes home and tells you about her softball exploits. Yet you know very well that she only gets to play in the last inning when her team is winning, that she can barely swing a bat, and that she has never hit the ball, let alone hit three home runs. You can say, "Boy, I can't tell if it's a story or if it really happened, but it sounds as though you would really like to be a hero or a star on the team. It seems to me that the story you told me really means that you wish you could hit a softball like that and get all those home runs. I think that's why you told me this, isn't it?" Your child might get angry and say, "Well, don't you believe me?"

Second Step

Do not nail her to the wall and say, "No, I don't!" Simply say, "I think it's hard for you to tell me that it may not have really happened. You wanted me to believe that you did all those great things. I really understand how important it is for you to feel that you could do these things, but I would rather know what actually happened."

Third Step

If your child is between three and five years old and is making up wild fantasies, she will usually respond favorably if you simply say, "It sounds as though you enjoy making up interesting stories about the things you would like to do, or how big and powerful you'd like to be. It's okay if you want to make up stories, but sometimes I'm going to ask you whether that's one of your fun stories or if it really happened."

Fourth Step

This step is for children who don't tell the truth because they want to get their own way. Suppose your child comes to you and says. "I've already done my homework, so can I watch TV?" When you find out the homework wasn't done, don't say to her through gritted teeth, "Why did you lie to me, you little varmint? I told you it's always better to tell me the truth!" Remember, you do not resort to this type of accusation anymore. Say to her instead, "I think you told me that you did your homework because you really wanted to watch TV, but you were afraid I wouldn't let you. Sometimes you tell me things because you want to have your way, but if you do that again, you will lose your privilege to watch TV."

Empathizing with your child also works. You may sometimes tell her, "You must have been worried that I'd really be upset or that you wouldn't get what you wanted. I know it's really hard to tell the truth, because I remember how hard it was for me when I was a kid. But if you don't tell the truth, I'll have to take some TV time away from you this evening."

Fifth Step

If you accuse your child of not telling the truth (or imply it), but you're not sure that you're right, you can say, "I think I'm right. But I want you to know that if I find out I'm wrong, I will apologize for not believing you." The day you say this, your child will probably keel over in shock because you said that you're willing to apologize. How often did your parents say that to you?

Sixth Step

Let your child know what the real issue is. Say, "My main concern is for you to learn that you don't have to worry so much if you do something wrong. I hope that next time you can tell me the truth so we can work out the problem." Work out the problem, not her lying. The problem is why did she have trouble in openly expressing her true feelings to you?

Seventh Step

Using the preceding approaches might induce your child to finally confess her little crime. Even if she admits to you two weeks later that she lied, don't say to her, "Why did it take you so long?" or, "I knew all along that you did it." I hope you'll say, "I really feel good that you told me, and maybe next time it won't be so hard to tell me sooner." This approach tells your child that you have some understanding of why it's so difficult to tell the truth. She understands by your attitude that the punishment is not some big, scary thing. Your child learns that it really isn't so unnerving to tell you the truth and that you aren't such a bad person after all.

You might be thinking, "This is a crazy man who's telling me that every time my kid makes up a story or exaggerates, I'm supposed to spend my days saying obnoxious things like, 'Gee, it was really hard for you to tell me the truth' or 'I understand, that it was really a story.' "

If your child has a pattern of getting locked into lying to you, then the preceding approaches are critically important. If she only does it periodically, the most important thing to do is not to make a big deal about it. In the normal development of children, they find less and less need to lie as they mature.

11

Stealing

Parents are frequently shocked when children take things from them, from the neighbors, stores, relatives, or friends. Starting at a very early age, children (sometimes as young as three) gleefully slip things into their pockets and then hide the items. Most mothers seem to find these well-hidden treasures.

Young children take things for the following reasons: (1) They simply want the item, and they see no reason in the world why they shouldn't have it. Young children want instant gratification, and they see no sensible excuse why they shouldn't have what they want—regardless of whether it's in a store or someone else's house. (2) An older child sees other children with the things that he doesn't have. He feels very jealous, and he wants the item because he has competitive feelings. (3) Occasionally, children take things as a way of expressing a wish to be close to a friend, parent, or relative. They actually take things from the people with whom they strongly identify.

This is the reason that children may sometimes take things from their parents. I'm not talking about ripping off a twenty-dollar bill from your wallet, but about when they take something that's very important to you and that they know is important. (4) On the other hand—just to muddle up this area more—taking something you value may be a good way of getting revenge or letting out anger toward someone. (5) Some children will steal things and then show the items to other people in order to get attention for having taken something special. Or, an older child may be letting others know that he's not afraid to do risky things. This makes him look big and powerful. No child steals because he is a born thief.

Kids will take things, hide them, rip them off . . . but I refuse to call it stealing until the pattern is consistent and persists into adolescence.

To deal with "stealing," you must understand your child's agenda. You must look for motives other than the obvious one.

First Step

We must bear in mind the principle that has been discussed in the chapter about lying. If you see your child take something, don't besiege him with the investigative approach. Just tell him that you saw him take the object or that you found out that he took it. Since it doesn't belong to him, tell him it has to be returned, whether it has been taken from a store, a school, or wherever. If you do this in an unemotional way and begin early in the child's life, he won't develop a sense of guilt. He may not feel terrible about being coerced to return the item and he shouldn't, because it is not a major crime for a child. Tell him, "Any time you take something that isn't yours, it will have to be returned, or it will be kept by Mom. Mom and Dad want you to learn to control yourself from taking things that do not belong to you. And if you can't control yourself, you'll have to go to bed earlier every time you take something. I know that you can learn to control yourself." By saying this, you give your child an important message: he must control himself.

Second Step

If your child likes to go to the store with you, you may have to tell him that if he can't stop taking things from the shelves, you will leave him at home next time. I understand that you may have to make special arrangements to organize this, but it is one way to teach your child not to take things. After enforcing this consequence a few times, you can tell him that you want to give him a chance to go to the store so he can show you that he's ready to be a big boy and not take things. Tell him that he may choose one item that you will buy for him if he learns to show control.

Third Step

If your child takes something from you but has rarely done so before, don't interrogate him when you ask him if he took it. If he says he didn't, then tell him that the item is important to you and you'd really like to have it back. In the event that it's hard for him to tell you about it, ask him to give it some thought. Now, if you have a strong suspicion that he took it, you can tell your child that if he thinks about it and he doesn't come up with the item, you might have to look through his things, because you're not sure he's telling the truth. And, again, you can tell him that if you're wrong, you will apologize to him, but you are really concerned about the item that you think he has taken. If you can do this in an unemotional way, matter-of-factly, you will raise some appropriate anxiety in your child, and he will realize you are serious but fair.

Fourth Step

If you find the item or if the child admits to you that he took it, again, it is important not to react. Say that it must have really been hard for him to tell you, and you hope that next time he'll realize that you can work these things out. Tell him, "This item must go back to the store. You will have to return it with me."

Fifth Step

Suppose your child is over five and he has taken something from a neighbor, a friend, or a store. By this age he has developed a sense of awareness or appropriate concern about taking things. You don't have to march your child across to the neighbor and force an apology.

For a child who rarely takes things, be fair and supportive. Say, "Since you admitted you took it, do you want me to take it back and tell them for you? This time, it will be OK because I know it's hard to do. Or, do you want to go with me and I will help you talk to them and tell them you're sorry? But you will have to take it back by yourself if you do it again, whether you want to or not."

The important aspect to remember about stealing and lying is that if you treat the issue in an emotionally nonthreatening way, and if you act as though it isn't any more serious than other behaviors, you will find that "stealing" is a phase your child will go through and one of which he will tire. Children basically don't have a need to "steal."

12

Hitting

Most parents don't like their children to hit, spit, or kick. They wonder if their child is weird, and they fantasize about sending her away somewhere until she won't need to display this behavior.

A parent's wish is for the child to sit down and discuss her problems in a reasonable, civilized manner even though adults sometimes find this difficult to do. It is important to note that a child's kicking, hitting, and spitting isn't any different than the emotional outburst of an adult. There are times when adults would like to kick, hit, and spit, but they are wise enough to know this is socially unacceptable.

The question is, how do we handle this behavior? Some people would say to hit your child back, or shake her so hard that she looks like she is made out of jelly. I'm not saying that this won't teach your child a hard lesson; sometimes it does. However, what it teaches her is that your aggression is more powerful than hers.

You might moralize to your child, telling her that children who spit and kick are doomed never to have any friends and only mean, terrible kids act like that. Maybe you're the kind of parent who tries to discuss with your child in an understanding way that she should stop her hitting-spitting-kicking behavior.

The important thing is to recognize that in normal development, some hitting, and even spitting and kicking, is an early expression of a child's wish for power, or an expression of anger, pain, and sometimes fear. Even a child as young as two may behave aggressively because of frustration and her lack of understanding of a situation.

As your child reaches about four years of age, much of her hitting and aggression is related to her wish for control over adults and other playmates while she is interacting with them. Her anger comes from not understanding that there are other ways to get what she wants, or how to deal with her feelings of frustration.

It should also be pointed out that children continue hitting because they feel extremely angry. Hitting is a way of releasing pent-up frustration. There may be a lack of permission to get angry at home, or the other extreme, too much permission, which will cause the child to feel frustrated when she doesn't get her way, and she strikes out because of her need for instant gratification. Additionally, if your child has been given her own way at home all the time, things are different when she goes to school and into social situations. She's going to find that others don't give in to her as her parents do. This often causes the child to feel frustrated, and then she becomes very aggressive. This is not good preparation for conflict resolution in the future. A child who is unprepared in this way will have difficulty resolving problems in the real world.

As I have discussed, during the preschool years, some physical aggression is a very normal way for children to deal with frustration, anger, and fear. If this is primarily the only way that your child deals with her frustration, you should be concerned enough to think that something is very wrong with her social/emotional development. An important thing to realize is that all of us have some primitive rage inside and we hope as we grow up that it takes a different form. Remember, though, that the behavior you might find socially unacceptable in your child is very similar to the behavior of adults. There are probably times when you would like to punch someone in the jaw or kick him in the shins. However, since you know that you can't justify expressing your rage in this manner, you resort to other techniques: very snide looks or remarks, gossiping in a nasty way, excluding your "enemy" from social events to "get back at him."

The point is we all have basic feelings of anger, and you must understand that your child is attempting to work out these feelings, which are appropriate in her growing years. Again, your attitude about her behavior is the significant issue. Obviously, if your kid kicks, hits, or spits, you must tell her that it is unacceptable behavior. But you also need to let her know that you understand why she can become angry and upset, and you should assure her that she is not committing a crime if it happens occasionally. You must help her learn to handle this another way. (If you give this area too much intensity, you are handing over too much power to her which may encourage her to act out the same behavior again.) You might also make your child feel extremely guilty, as though she's done something horrible, rather than something lots of children do now and then. So, the attitude is to be firm but to let your child know it's unacceptable to hit.

Here are some steps you can take if your child persists in hitting and none of the preceding suggestions have been effective in dealing with the problem.

First Step

Tell your child, "I know I've gotten mad at you for hitting your brother [sister] and I'm going to have to find another way to help you with this problem. You can't keep doing this. I know it might be hard to stop, because you get very mad inside when you're feeling upset. But I have some new rules that you will have to try instead of hitting."

Second Step

Say, "If you're feeling very mad, come to me and tell me you're angry. We can let you hit a pillow, scream, talk about what made you so upset, or find some way to get this out of your system instead of hurting someone. When you feel yourself becoming angry, I want you to think about something you can do to get your feelings out without hurting someone. They you can try to stop the hitting and spitting before it happens. I know that's not easy to do. All I'm asking you to do is try."

Third Step

If your child is unable to do this, you tell her, "It's so important to your Mom and me that you learn to stop doing this. There's going to be a consequence if you can't learn to control yourself. Every time you hit or kick there will be more time taken away from your playtime until you learn to control yourself. If I see that you're trying and that you're doing better, I won't always take time away from you. This is because I will see that you are really trying."

When you are empathetic but firm, you make your child's struggle easier when she is learning different ways to control herself. You're also telling her that you understand that she is struggling to regain self-control.

13

Four-letter Words

Now, of course, *your* children don't ever say anything like "caca-poo," "silly butt," "do-do," or "poop!" Only the bad kids down the street talk like that, right? Not true. Most children start using these words a little after the age of three. Then they graduate to words that make you want to dive under tables, roll up your car windows, and avoid your friends for a month. The first time you hear your child use the "F" word or copy one of Dad's favorite cuss words, you'll probably feel like moving to Siberia.

Once again, you may fear that your child will use these words as a regular part of his vocabulary. He is discovering and testing the power of words. Words make parents and friends giggle, turn red, get embarrassed, or holler with rage. With his peers, the right words will get him attention, make his friends laugh, and give permission for the other children to express their aggressive feelings.

You are teaching your child that he has power over you when you fall apart at his verbiage and ask. "Where in the world did you learn that?" or, "Where did you get that filthy mouth?" You forgot that the last time you cut yourself you yelled, "Oh, damn it, that hurts!"

You cue children into their behavior. Once your child sees that these four-letter words elicit a variety of very interesting responses, he figures, "why not use them?" "If a dumb little word evokes such a strong reaction," your child may say to himself, "I can really have a lot of fun. Everyone goes crazy when I say these strange things, and I don't even know what they mean. But, boy, do they work!"

As your child gets older, he learns that these words have implications of social disapproval. Still, they also continue to have a certain amount of power when expressed.

Don't shoot me for what I am about to say, but the initial use of these words definitely has some value in your child's development. As suggested, it teaches him about the use of emotional, expressive words, how much power they have, and how to express hostility. When you as a parent react, these words teach him that there are ways to get back at you. They also give your child permission to express words related to sexual feelings. Because many socially unacceptable words obviously have meaning to him and this is the beginning of his awareness of sexuality in himself and others, expressing them out loud is one way of dealing with his normal interest in this area.

Verbal aggression of this sort does not indicate budding sexual perversion.

Let's focus on your behavior when your child uses "bad" words. You probably get embarrassed and drill your kid with laser-beam glares. You might utter very quickly, "You're really going to get it when you get home." This makes him very uncomfortable, and if he's the type who acts out his emotions, he'll probably say the word one more time just to let you know that the laser-beam approach won't work because he thinks he is Superman. It is wise to ignore this last attempt of defiance.

You might be an old-fashioned parent who is convinced that the best approach to four-letter words is washing your kid's mouth out with soap. I'm not going to tell you that washing his mouth out with soap won't stop him from using cuss words, because on occasion I have known children who take two good swallows and decide it's not worth it to use those words again. However, it's not an approach that I would suggest. I don't think that it teaches a child much except for the fact that you found a punishment that makes him massively uncomfortable. He'll only learn from this because he is fearful that you'll punish him like that again.

The most notorious response is the Morality Approach. You tell your child at an early age that he's going to grow up to be one of the most disgusting human beings on earth and that nobody will like him or care about him if he uses these words. Particularly when he's young, he will find out that these words have little impact on whether he is liked or disliked by his peers, unless all he does is cuss and act socially inappropriately. What you're doing is trying to sell him on a morality that has little meaning to him.

First Step

Understand that children between three and five are trying words on for size. At first it is better not to react to the use of four-letter words; try to ignore them. As the child gets older, he will use these words for all the reasons previously mentioned. Many times your child will lose interest because he's attained the maximum mileage from the giggles and shock.

Second Step

If you try to ignore it and your child still persists, it's time to move on. Say to him, "I know you like to use these words, but I've heard them enough. So, if you need to use them, I want you to say them as many times as you want to in your room. When you come out, though, you will have to stop using them. If you can't control yourself when you come out, you will have to spend a longer time in your room until you're tired of saying these words."

Isolating your child is effective because, to a kid, it's no fun to use these words when nobody can hear them. By sending him to his room, you are taking away the pleasure he gets when he uses these words in front of people. And when you do this, his behavior will usually change rather quickly.

Third Step

This step is for the child who persists. The trick is to make something positive out of something negative. Instead of saying, "I told you not to say that word," try, "I can see that you're doing better, even though you just used one of the words we talked about. But you haven't been saying them as much."

This is easier to do if you are at home and not out in public. Sometimes, if your child is young and you are out in public, you can say to him. "Remember what the rule is: if you need to use those words, you can say them in your room at home. But I don't want you to say them in the store or with your friends." If your child asks why, you don't have to say because it's not nice or because people won't like you. Just tell him that this is one of your rules. Remember, you're the parent and he's the kid.

Fourth Step

If your child is older and you're out in public, explain to him that he doesn't have to use "those" words in public. If he continues, tell him, "If you can't control what you're saying, you will have to go to bed early when you get home."

For example, your child is in the car or in someone's house and you keep hearing cuss words. You let him know that he has said those words enough, and there will be a consequence when you get home.

Fifth Step

If he tests you by saying the words again, tell him that he will go to bed ten minutes earlier if he keeps it up. In other words, give the increased consequence with a warning.

Or, if your child is in someone's house or in a store, you can immediately tell him that because he couldn't stop talking in an unacceptable manner, he will have to go home at once. Remember, the issue is the persistent behavior. You have to show him that his behavior is important enough for you to leave the store or your friend's house in order to enforce a consequence. Remember, also, that you know what kind of consequence has meaning to your child, because you've been a good observer, and you've been consistent in your approach. As you can see, the same themes underlie all of the approaches that have been discussed, regardless of the specific situation.

You must continue to impress upon your child that his behavior is all-important to you and that you intend to do your job. At the same time, you must be careful not to reveal any hypersensitivity about the issue of four-letter words. Remember, your child's agenda is to test his power and your authority. It only appears that he's trying to ruin your social standing.

PART V
CHILDREN'S EMOTIONAL ISSUES

14

Crises for Children

Crises for children and adults have some common components: they create feelings that most of us are uncomfortable with. The difference may be how the adults and children handle them. These crises include death, divorce, illness, and major life changes such as moving and going to a new school. We are all familiar with these critical turning points, but over and over I hear parents say that they don't know how to talk to their children about them. A common remark is, "She must not miss her dad because she hasn't said a thing yet and her dad's been gone for two months. That makes me feel better because I couldn't stand him anyway." From this we see that some parents believe that if a child hasn't said anything, she doesn't feel anything.

When there's a crisis, your child's behavior may vary from talking incessantly about it, to acting as if nothing's different at all. Any response she makes is an attempt to deal with something that is extremely painful for her.

On the other hand, your child may deal with these issues by denying her feelings. She may become angry or sullen if you ask her about the death, divorce, or change, or she may worry unduly over any change in her life. She might think that if she had been nicer to Grandma she wouldn't have died, or if she hadn't screamed at Dad he wouldn't have left. In other words, your child is trying to make sense of this confusion.

In all of the major crises—death, divorce, and illness—the common concerns your child has are the following: Is someone to blame? What's going to happen to my world? How do I make everything OK? Will my parents be all right?

ILLNESS

When speaking of illness, I am talking primarily about those unusual situations when someone in your family has to go to the hospital or has a prolonged illness at home. I am assuming that this person will recover. Your child will usually become very anxious, and even sometimes angry, when seeing someone whom she associates with strength come home feeling weak. Generally, this is because she is afraid for your well-being as well as her own. She may also have unusual fantasies about illness. For example, if her uncle has a heart attack and then your child sees something that frightens her, she will associate illness with something scary. Or, your child might feel the need to take on a helping role, doing as much as she can to assist in the relative's recuperation. To a certain extent the child's attempt to help gives her a sense of control. It is important to remember that she is worried and is trying to deal with her feelings of concern.

First Step

Let your child know by saying "Honey, if Dad goes to the hospital for an operation, he may not feel very strong right away, but he will be OK. Dad won't look any different when he returns, but he will be a little tired. He will not be able to throw you up in the air the way he used to until he feels better, and he will need more quiet, so you will have to cooperate."

Second Step

Reassure your child that you can handle this problem, that Mom will take care of things while Dad is in the hospital. Tell your child that the two of you will be able to get along fine, even though everyone will miss Dad until he comes home. Here, a great deal of reassurance is appropriate.

Third Step

Prepare your child for the length of time her dad will be gone. She should be told when she can regularly telephone him in the hospital. Even if Dad feels weak when she calls, she should be reassured that he is getting better but that it will take time. If possible, it's good to prepare your child in advance for her dad's homecoming by setting up a chart or a calendar. This way she will know when she can talk to him, and when she'll be able to see him. This gives your child a feeling of control.

Fourth Step

Tell your child that sometimes Mom or Dad (whichever parent is not in the hospital) may seem weepy and sad. Explain that you know your spouse will be fine, but be aware that your child may show delayed reactions when seeing your vulnerabilities. Keep in mind that she may not show any reaction, but she's probably feeling nervous and scared.

Fifth Step

Use this step if it becomes necessary. Let's say Grandma is ill and you don't know if she will be OK. You can't reassure your child that everything will be fine when she asks about her. You should still use all of the preceding techniques except for the following modification. Say, "I know you're asking me this because you're worried about Grandma. So am I. The doctors are trying to help her the best way they can, and they will let us know how she is doing. We know you're worried. So are we." This will reassure many children. If your child persists and asks, "Is Grandma going to die?" you have to be honest. If it's a serious illness, tell her, "We don't know, but we're hoping for the best for her. I know it makes you feel bad that we're not sure if Grandma will be all right. But she might die, and that makes all of us feel bad." Remember to tell your child that she can come to you if she needs to talk about it again. Tell her you know how hard it is for her to think about it.

DEATH

Typically, death is a subject we don't like to think about as adults. Somehow, the subject becomes even more threatening when it must be explained to children. As an adult, you might have a difficult time defining what you feel and think about death. It's important to note that, on some level, your child will pick up your discomfort. When I work with parents and I suggest that they discuss the subject with their child who isn't showing any adverse reactions to a recent death, I hear, "Why should I upset my child?" Yes, you will probably cause her to feel some discomfort. However, if you can encourage her to share her confusion and discomfort about this issue, it is the beginning of her awareness of this very painful issue of life.

Many children show delayed reactions to death months after the event. Your child might start worrying about you and your spouse when you go out at night. She may show symptoms and concerns about her own body and express excessive concern about the well-being of people close to her.

To help your child integrate her feelings about death, here are some concrete suggestions.

First Step

You should not expect your child to have a serious discussion about death. This type of conversation will unnecessarily frighten and burden her. You might introduce the subject when playing a game or simply when you're together. You might say, "I want you to listen to something I have been meaning to tell you. You don't have to answer me, Honey, it will be all right if you just listen to me." When you start this way, you give your child premission not to respond to you. You then tell her in a very limited conversation (remember that most children won't sit for twenty minutes and discuss this) that you have been feeling sad since Grandma died, and if she sees you around the house looking sad or crying, it's because you're feeling sad about it. Tell her that you need to get your feelings out, and you'll feel better after you do. This gives her permission to express her feelings.

Now, if someone has just died, you might start off by keeping the same ideas in mind. Say, "I need to tell you that Grandma just died, and it's sad for me. This news might be hard for you to hear. If you'd like to talk about it now or you just want a hug, that's fine. If you don't feel you can, that's OK, too. If you see me feeling sad, it's because this is a very hard time for me and your father [or your mother]. But we're all going to be OK, and we will help you to be OK."

Second Step

Remember to periodically ask your child how she's feeling about Grandma's death. This means that every few weeks for the first few months you should make a statement in the following manner, "I'm feeling a little better but I still feel sad that Grandma died. I wonder if you are feeling a little bit better, too, or are you feeling just as sad as before?" If your child says, "No, I'm not feeling sad, I'm mad," you say, "I can understand that because you want her back with us."

If your child is under six years old, sometimes she will have a hard time knowing what dying is. You must explain, "It means we won't see Grandma anymore because when a person gets very, very old and they've lived a long time, their body doesn't work any more. This happens when we all get very old. I'm not old and your mommy [or daddy] isn't old, so our bodies—and yours—will work for a very long time. Remember, Grandma didn't walk very well and she had a hard time doing small things so she had to rest a lot. That's what happens when your body isn't working too well, and finally it can't work at all."

Generally, at this age your child is not going to ask about exceptions to the rule. But if he asks, and if a classmate has died, say, "I know that Mary died when she was seven years old, but that doesn't usually happen. She had an illness most children never get. Daddy, your brother, you, and I are not likely to get sick like that. Remember that all of your classmates are OK except for Mary."

Continue by saying, "If you want to talk more about this, when you feel like it, Mom and Dad will be glad to listen to you."

Third Step

Remember, if your child asks you questions that you can't answer specifically, it is OK to say, "I don't know." Lots of questions from her usually means she is worrying about the death. You should say, "I guess you're asking these questions because you still feel bad about Grandma." The point is that many specific questions relate much more to your child's feelings than to the need to have a specific answer. Give her a hug, a reassuring word, a special story at bedtime, anything to show your understanding.

DIVORCE

What we are essentially dealing with in this chapter is response to loss. Frequently parents do not realize the impact a divorce has on a child. A child may experience a divorce as if her whole world is falling apart, and she doesn't know how to put it back together.

The main issues concerning divorce are: who caused it? (so blame can be put somewhere); the fantasy wish of bringing the parents back together; anger at the parents for messing up the child's life; the worry about how and when she will be able to see the absent parent; and the question: "Is it OK to love both parents the same way since the divorce?"

If you are not enraged with one another, and you can behave decently, your job of explaining will be easier. When you, as parents, have made a decision to get a divorce, both of you should sit down with your child in a comfortable setting. This could even be one in which she is playing. You may have to do this several times, because she might do everything from acting silly to saying things like, "I don't want to talk about this dumb thing!"

First Step

Tell your child, "We can't live together any more because we don't get along." If your child says, "I don't want to hear this silly stuff," or acts nutty, you say, "I know that you're acting this way because it's hard for you to hear, and I know it's hard to talk about." If either parent cries, say, "I'm crying because this is sad and it is hard for me, but I'll be OK. If you feel like crying, it's OK." Continue by saying, "We have tried to work out our problems, but we can't do it, so we need to live away from each other. We wish we could have worked out our difficulties, but we haven't been able to."

Second Step

Tell your child, "This is our problem, and it's not because of anything that you have done. Our divorce doesn't change the fact that we both love you very much. Sometimes adults do things that can make their children feel mixed up. But even if you feel mixed up, we are going to get a divorce."

Third Step

Explain: "We'll understand if this makes you mad at us or if you feel sad because we feel that way, too."

Fourth Step

Reassure your child that the absent parent is not abandoning her. Say, "You're still going to see Mom [or Dad] a lot, and we'll set up regular times to visit. Mom [or Dad] has a new place where she [or he] will be living. We will work out schedules with you. We want you to know that even when she [or he] leaves, she [or he] is still your mom [or your dad] just like before, and you can count on that. It will be different because Mom [or Dad] won't be home every day. This may be difficult for a while—not seeing each other every day—but I think we can both get used to it."

Remember, your child may not be able to listen to all of this at once. So, if you talk about the divorce a little bit at a time, she will gradually be able to accept talking about it.

FEELING BAD ABOUT DIVORCE

Hopefully, one or both parents, separately, will do the following.

First Step

Say to your child, without your spouse being present, "You know that your dad, and I aren't living together, and you could see that we were very mad at each other when he left. I know that it must have been scary and it made you unhappy. It's not your fault. Even though your dad and I are mad at each other, I want you to know that he loves you very much. I understand that you still love him, even though we're apart."

Second Step

Say, "I don't want you to blame your dad for leaving or to think that he's wrong and I'm right."

Third Step

"Your dad and I may not be able to be nice to each other, but I hope we can try when we do see each other. I hope we can get over this so it won't be so hard on you."

Fourth Step

"If your dad and I make you feel too bad, you can tell us and that's OK. Even if you feel scared or mad, you need to tell us that."

Fifth Step

"Remember, when you're with Dad, you may be able to do many things that are more fun than when you are with me. He may take you to different places because he isn't with you every day. I won't be able to do that as much even though you may want me to. So it might seem to be more fun with Dad."

The following should be indicated to your child: "Your dad is feeling very upset, and he is having difficulty spending time with you. It's not your fault, and you're not to blame for making him feel that way. It's because we are getting a divorce. I don't think he is trying to hurt you, but he's so unhappy that he can't be the kind of parent you and I would like him to be. I know this is hard and it mixes you up, but you need to know that we aren't certain if he is going to be able to do it. I will take care of you and make sure that things are OK with you."

I realize that some parents, when struggling with each other, don't feel like giving any credit to the other parent. If you realize that your concern is for your child, you must be fair—no matter how bad you feel toward your former spouse. Yes, my statement is intended to provoke your sense of responsibility. Divorce is so painful for your child that you truly must put your feelings in a secondary position at least some of the time. This is the only way for her to learn to live with this very difficult life change.

15

Permission for Feelings

EMOTIONS THAT DRIVE PARENTS CRAZY

For years children were to be seen and not heard. "Respect your parent" was the watchword of the day. Behavior such as screaming, crying, and foot stomping, which expressed "negative" feelings like anger, defiance, and irritability, were clearly unacceptable. In many families, children did not openly express such emotions to their parents. Children sometimes express themselves in unacceptable ways when they lose control. In the past, many parents' reactions to this were quite clear; feelings that threatened absolute parental authority were unacceptable.

Fortunately, today most parents now understand that a child needs to express his feelings—positive or negative. Sometimes the manner of expression is infuriating to the parent. It seems that no matter how modern you try to be, your child's expression of emotion leaves you frustrated. A solution can be to allow the emotion but set limits for its expression. Sometimes we professionals have compounded the issue by overemphasizing how good it is for kids to express themselves. But we don't help to clarify the acceptable boundaries of children's expressions. Children need to know what the acceptable and unacceptable ways are to let out anger and frustration. They need help with this because their experience (when young) is limited, much of the time, to reacting. The parents' job is to clarify this issue for their children and to let them know that they may express many things that are acceptable, while others are not.

For example, if your child repeatedly expresses anger with swear words or constantly whines, this is unacceptable. On the other hand, an occasional (but not habitual) strong reaction should be accepted as a normal reaction. As a parent, you should say in a firm but understanding tone, "You really must have been upset to use those words. You must find another way to talk to me when you're angry. But, now let's talk about what upset you."

If, because you are unprepared, you lose control when responding, you may go back to your child and say, "I got mad when you talked that way to me, but I realize you must have been upset." This is observant behavior on your part. Now let's discuss the emotions that give the most difficulty.

ANGER

Children's attempts to express normal feeling can sometimes sound like verbal attacks on their parents. Statements a parent might hear are, "You're a dummy face," "I hate you—I wish you weren't my mommy" or "You're the meanest mommy on earth." A typical parental response would be "Don't you dare talk to me like that!" or "Take that nasty look off your face!" To this day, kids haven't been able to figure out how to take a look off their faces. Another frequent parental response is, "How dare you talk to me like that after all I've done for you? I give you everything you want, and then you treat me like this!" As they get older, kids will mumble statements under their breath like, "I hate you." A parent will often respond with, "What did you say?" to which the child naturally replies, "Nothing." None of these often-heard comments will change your child's behavior. You might feel temporarily better after you've made one because your child acts guilty, but it never teaches him anything constructive.

Like it or not, we usually express anger at the people we feel safe with. So when you think your kid really has it in for you, he may also be telling you that he feels safe enough with you to let out some of his frustrations. (I'm sure this comment will make you love your child's anger from this day on.) OK, now what do we do about it?

First Step

Notice what angers your child. Is it when he doesn't get his way or when he can't do something he'd like to do? Is it when his feelings have been hurt or when he's disappointed?

Second Step

If your child responds to you in a negative, angry manner, reflect his feelings in this way, "Boy, I can see you're telling me this in an angry way because you're so upset that this happened or you're upset with me. You know, you can tell me that you're angry, but you're going to have to tell me in another way. You can say, 'Dad, I'm mad at you' or 'Dad, I don't like you now.' So it's OK to be angry, but I won't listen to it if you're screaming and yelling and acting out of control."

Third Step

Talk to your child during a quiet moment, perhaps at bedtime after a good day. "Honey, I know Mom has talked to you about being so angry, and you still seem so angry. Maybe I act that way with you. I would like to tell you in a nice voice when you sound like that. And you can tell me, too, when I sound angry. This way we can learn to feel better about each other."

Fourth Step

This is an option you can give your child if he cannot talk out his anger. "If you can't tell me what is bothering you and you need to express your anger, you can hit a pillow or throw a ball up against the garage door. That will help you get your anger out."

Fifth Step

Use this step if none of the above has worked and you have become locked into a struggle. Your child may need firm limits rather than permission for expression. Some children need to learn to control their emotions because they tend to flood out their feelings. When your child continues with his angry reactions, you can respond in the following manner. "You still get too mad when I tell you to do something, so I will have to teach you better control another way. It's OK to tell me you're mad and that you don't always like to listen to me. But it's not acceptable for you to go on screaming and yelling at me. If you're unable to control this every time I ask you to do something, you will lose fifteen minutes of your playtime (or another consequence). If you still have trouble controlling yourself, the next time you act this way, it will be half an hour off playtime." Remember, you add additional time to the consequence so that your child truly realizes that he loses more by his behavior than you do. Next, you can say, "I hope you control yourself so you don't lose the things that are important to you. I really want to work this out with you. I would rather not have to make this rule, but I will do this until you learn to get in control."

You are showing your child that you will be firm, will clarify what is expected of him, and will continue to work on his behavior until he learns to control himself.

CRYING

Children need permission to cry. Crying is a healthy outlet. They should know that feeling upset, sad, or overwhelmed, and releasing such feelings by crying is very permissible and understandable. It is only when kids use this method over and over as the only outlet for frustration that parents need to help the child get in control.

Children obviously cry for many reasons. Children between the ages of one and three cry when they're frustrated, can't get their way, feel misunderstood, or are fearful or confused. If a child is crying because something really frightened or confused him, or he is startled, we should handle this situation in a very supportive, warm, loving manner. Even if a child is somewhat older—around four years old and up—his crying under these circumstances tells us he needs considerable support and understanding regarding these particular situations. Generally parents know what to do when a child becomes fearful over these incidents, but it's important to point out what not to do. Some children cry over everything; they need help to learn control.

Don't ask your child why he's crying, tell him that he has nothing to cry about, or tell him that he's getting upset over nothing. This usually increases crying rather than decreasing it. A parent who does this not only is a bad observer of the impact she has on the child but also hasn't learned that children have a right to feel this way under certain circumstances.

First Step

If a child is crying over and over because of his immaturity, holding him in a firm and warm way is one way of helping him to cope. Don't cuddle the child, because that only reinforces his sense of helplessness. Standing right next to him and holding him with your arm around him, say, "I'm holding you because I care that you feel bad. But you need to get in control. You can learn to do this."

Second Step

Firmly and softly, tell your child, "I can see that you are really scared, but you're going to be OK. I am going to help you calm down." After you say this a few times, you then say, "I really want you to try to get in control now because you don't have to be afraid any more." Obviously, we are not talking about a traumatic situation that your child couldn't get over immediately, such as death or divorce. These are the situations that sometimes need professional help.

If a child cries because he's frustrated or because he didn't get his way, don't say, "Stop that crying." Once you have identified that he has this pattern and you're locked into it, use some of the steps discussed below concerning whining.

Third Step

Say, "I know you're crying because you didn't get to stay longer at your friend's house. I really understand that it's hard, but I want you to try to gain control of yourself."

Fourth Step

State the third step once or twice and don't go on until you see that your child is trying to get in control. Then say, "I can see that you're trying to control yourself and I'm really proud of you."

Fifth Step

If your child is unable to gain control, tell him ahead of time (before the next crying bout), "I know you've had trouble getting in control when you don't get your own way or when you're upset. I have tried to help you by letting you know that you must try and stop yourself. So far, this hasn't helped you, so from now on we have a new rule: when you need to cry over these things, you have to do it in your room until you're finished. When you feel that you are ready to stop, I'll let you come out. If you can stop yourself, you won't have to go to your room."

Sixth Step

If your child has tried to control himself by going to his room, comment to him that you can see he is really trying and that he is doing much better. Tell him you really believe he can gain control. In this way you're telling your child that you believe in his potential to gain control, and you don't think he's doomed to spend the rest of his life flooding the world with tears.

If your child is over six years old, the steps I've outlined still apply. Some of the time you'll be able to have a discussion with him. You could talk about some of the reasons he gets so frustrated and upset. At a warm moment between parent and child, you want to have a conversation something like this: "I know things have been hard for you lately because you've been crying a lot and you're upset most of the time. Let's think of a way together that can help you to calm down. Is there anything that we haven't talked about that I can do that might help you? If you feel that you are ready now or you will be sometime later, think about this, and I'll see what I can do to help you." Some parents who are locked in might be saying, "What's this guy talking about? I haven't had one of those 'good' moments with my kid in five years. When would I ever be able to bring all that up?" Well, let's give it a try anyway.

Sometimes, without sending your child to his room and without using consequences, he will understand, and he will try a lot harder. This is especially true if you say things like. "I will try not to look so upset at you when you cry or when you get frustrated. I realize that sometimes I don't help you very much by doing this."

Some children become moody and irritable, which indicates that they haven't learned to deal with the problems they must face when they get older. Finding a better way to express themselves emotionally will help them develop mature behavior. If a child uses crying as a way of expressing emotions (as opposed to being able to talk about his hurts and frustrations) or if he can't accept rules and regulations without crying, the procedures we've discussed are very important.

WHINING

Whining is prevalent between the ages of two and six. If your child whines, it is probably driving you mad. Your reaction only increases the whining. Most parents can't stand the sound or the look on their child's face when he whines. You feel quite helpless because you are unable to stop him from doing it. It makes you feel very frustrated and irritated.

Your child's agenda is an attempt to express a need that is being displayed in a regressive manner. He is inadequately trying to express anger, frustration, and a desire to be treated like a baby, because that used to feel so good. The more simple, obvious reason, if you look carefully, is that your child may be tired at the end of the day, and he may not be up to expressing himself cogently and effectively.

Basically, when your child whines, he is unable to express what he wants in a more appropriate manner. When you've been locked into this behavior, the typical comments are, "Stop it, you're driving me crazy. Why do you do this to me? I told you I can't stand it! Stop that noise or I'm going to blow my lid." He gets, understandably, attention every time he does this, even though it is negative. You're going to begin observing now, to see if you can break this pattern.

First Step

Observe your child's pattern. When does he whine? Is it when he's tired or when he doesn't get his way? Is it when he feels needy and may just want a hug?

Second Step

Talk to your child when he's not whining and tell him that you want to help him learn how to tell you what he needs instead of whining. Once you observe, you can say to him, "I can see that you whine when I tell you to do something you don't want to do. You can try to tell me with regular words instead of whining. I really know you can do this. But, we're still going to get the job done." Basically, you're asking your child to act appropriately for his age.

Third Step

When you see that your child is starting to whine, say to him, "Now see, you're starting to get upset. I want you to try to control yourself." If you see *any* effort, say, "Good, you're trying!" Later, say, "I think it was a lot better for you when you tried to control your whining, and I know you're going to learn how to feel better."

Fourth Step

Another way is to say to your child, "If you can stop whining, in a few minutes you can come in, and we'll pick a special game for us to play when I'm done with my work." Or "We'll do something special for awhile, if you try to control yourself."

Fifth Step

If your child is unable to stop, say, "I guess you're not ready to control yourself. If you need to whine, I want you to finish it in your room. When you're ready to stop, you can come out." Remember, when you are in this situation and the whining doesn't stop, you will have to make every effort to ignore it.

If you're not at home and your child whines in public, alter the fifth step as follows:

"If you can't control yourself and stop whining right now, you will have to spend time in your room to help you remember that you must be in control in public. I will give you one minute to try to stop whining."

Sixth Step

As soon as you see *any* change in your child's effort to control himself, say, "I can see that you're really trying and I'm proud of you." Or, as soon as he comes out of his room, say, "See, you can really do it. I knew you could." This is an appropriate time to give him a hug. Using a child's room is an effective consequence because it isn't any fun to be confined by yourself when you're crying and whining.

TANTRUMS

From early infancy through about four years old, children may express themselves by throwing tantrums. The child may throw himself on the floor (or whatever's available), flailing his arms and legs, and screaming at the top of his lungs. Another type of tantrum is the one in which a child gets very angry in an aggressive way and may try to hit or throw things. This is particularly embarrassing in front of friends, in markets, or in a restaurant. This is when you usually dart your eyes around, looking for a side door through which you can exit. You might command that your child, "Stop it!" You might try begging, bribery, or blackmail. All of these approaches generally increase the tantrum. We'll talk about how to deal with these issues in the following paragraphs.

At two, a tantrum is appropriate. Childrens' tolerance for frustration is limited at this age. They think everything should belong to them and can't figure out why they can't have exactly what they want when they want it. For example, if you tell your child it's time to go home when he's having the time of his life, you make absolutely no sense to him. Why should he have to stop? If he looks around, he sees no discernible reason why he can't play endlessly.

If a child is around four years of age and is still having tantrums regularly, it means he hasn't found a better way to deal with frustration and anger. Sometimes appropriate limits haven't been set on his behavior earlier. He may also be struggling with feelings that he can't talk about. In either case, immature behavior will be the result.

First Step

This step applies if your child has tantrums at home. If you have made a request of him that causes a tantrum and he does not become physically aggressive, first you should ignore him. Physically walk away saying, "When you regain control, I will come back and help you." As your child becomes quieter, say, "Good, you're trying to control yourself." If he becomes more irritated (sometimes any attention will have this effect), give him another chance to stop. Then say to him, "I know you had a hard time because you were so upset, and I want to give you a hug." You should do this even if it is twenty minutes later.

You still have to be consistent, and he still has to follow the rules. You might then say, "But we still have to clean up your room, and I'm going to help you get started."

Second Step

When things have calmed down and you and your child are having a good moment together, say to him, "I really want to help you learn not to get so upset when I ask you to do things. So, we're going to have to work on this together."

Third Step

If this positive approach isn't effective, you then have to speak to your child before another tantrum starts. In a very empathetic but firm way, say, "I've tried to help you understand that you must follow the rules without making a fuss. From now on, every time you can't control yourself, I'm going to put you in your room until you're finished screaming. This will teach you control." Remember to increase the amount of time he must spend in his room if the tantrum continues.

AGGRESSIVE TANTRUMS

When your child has aggressive tantrums, your method should be slightly different.

First Step

Tell your child he will have to learn another way to express himself when he's upset. He can't throw things around the house, or knock things over, or hit. When he does, he will have to go to his room until he's in control. If he comes out and he does it again, he will have to go to his room for a longer period of time.

Incidentally, if you try this and your child comes out of his room before he's gained control, you must teach him that you're very serious. You will have to put all other priorities aside. You may have to sit by the door to show him you mean what you say. You will have to keep him in his room until he's under control. Sometimes, if you walk away, your child might come out of his room five or six times, and then *you* may lose control. Tell him that you will not have to stand by the door and hold it when he shows you that he can stay in his room.

Discuss this procedure in a firm but concerned manner during a moment of rapport with your child. Tell him you feel bad for him and you know he needs help learning to control himself. Again, if you have become upset with him over the tantrum issue, tell him that since you don't like getting upset, you will try to stop.

Second Step

Say to your child, "You know that sometimes you're not going to like it when I have to send you to your room. But it's more important that you learn to gain control, even though you will probably get mad at me for doing this." You also say to him, "If you knock things over in your room, you know you will have to pick them up and organize the room again. That's part of the rule, too."

If you let your child hear this in a firm, calm tone, when you're feeling good, he has a chance to think about it and understand that you're trying to help him. He also sees that you can be positive and caring. It gives him time to try to get himself together. That's why it's so important to (1) observe your behavior and then, (2) talk about these issues effectively while in an unrelated situation.

If your child has a tantrum in public, your choices are clear but limited. You must immediately remove him from a restaurant or a market and put him in the car. Tell him he has to regain control or you're going home. If he doesn't, take him home and use the procedure discussed above. The important thing is that you are showing your child that you will remove him immediately from a situation where he's creating a scene and making you feel uncomfortable and embarrassed.

In this way, he learns immediately that this behavior will not get him what he wants. For example, if you told him that he couldn't buy another toy in the store or run around in the restaurant, make sure that he doesn't get the toy or continue running around. Also, you must be ready to delay the gratification you were having at the moment, such as eating your meal or finishing shopping. By doing this, you can teach your child that his behavior will not have the power to control you.

SNOTTY TALK

Around seven years of age, some children develop what I call a "snotty attitude." A parent will hear things like, "Do you have to bother me so much?" "Can't you see I'm on the phone?" "I'm busy!" The child might say in front of a neighbor, "Come on, Mom, stop talking and do this for me now!"

This is the time you want to dive under a table or say something like, "I've had it! Don't talk to me like that! Who do you think you are?" and, "If you ever do that in front of Mrs. Jones again, you'll really get it!"

However, your child's agenda is to get his own way. Also, he's trying to tell you something about the relationship. When parents are locked into these struggles, they sometimes really don't believe that their child is treating them badly. Parents tell themselves that the behavior will go away if they ignore it. Sometimes, by not being observant, parents are unaware that their child is frequently speaking with a nasty tone.

I feel that the child's behavior occurs because he regards the parent as if the adult is on the same level as the child's peers. This can result when parents try to be friends with their children, thereby relinquishing parental authority. The parent has not been aware and has ignored snotty talk, laughing it off as if it were normal.

Sometimes the snotty attitude occurs when a child feels depressed and unhappy, and he becomes irritable. Therefore, his tone and attitude take the form of snottiness. Whether or not this is the case, the parent can start by saying, "If you're talking like this because you are upset, I'll be glad to listen and talk with you. But I won't let you keep talking to me this way. You'll have to learn to control yourself, and I'll help you. I will try to understand when you are feeling bad."

If the behavior is not the result of unhappiness, the following section is a helpful way to attempt to handle it.

First Step

Tell your child that you have noticed for some time that he has been talking to you in a bossy, irritated tone, and that you are going to help him learn to speak in an improved manner. You can bring it to his attention by saying, firmly but understandingly, "You're using that tone of voice again. I want you to talk to me in a different way." If your child responds well, say, "That really is a lot easier to listen to, and I like the fact that you are trying."

Second Step

If the child has not improved, the parent can say, "I've tried to tell you in a nice voice about changing your tone and your nasty look. I will not answer anything that you request until you are ready to talk to me in another way. You'll have to decide when you're ready, but if you want anything, you must change your attitude. As soon as you change your tone, I will be glad to listen to your request, if I think it's fair." Parents should try not to hold onto their anger over this.

Third Step

If the child's attitude still has not changed, the parent must bring up the subject of consequences. Tell him, "If you keep talking like that, I want you to go to your room until you can decide to be in a different mood. If you choose to stay in your room all evening because of this, that's up to you. I hope you choose to change your attitude so you can come out of your room, because I'd like to spend an enjoyable evening with you."

Fourth Step

The parent says, "If this doesn't help, I'll decide how long you have to stay in your room. I will increase your time until you learn to change your attitude. But as long as I see that you are trying, and if you stop when I tell you to stop, then you won't have to go to your room."

Fifth Step

Sometimes the child will have a "snotty" attitude in front of other people. In that case, the parent should say, "One of the things I don't like about your manner is that you behave boorishly in front of anyone, not just me. If you can't learn to control yourself, I will have to say to them, 'Johnny sometimes talks like that because he hasn't learned to restrain himself.' I will have to tell them about the problem you have." When you do this, you put appropriate pressure on the child by embarrassing him for his inappropriate behavior. This is one of the rare times I suggest embarrassing a child, but when you are locked into a struggle over a child's "snotty" talk and attitude, sometimes this has to be done. Mom can say, "I prefer not to do this in front of other people, but I'll do it until you learn to change. I really hope you can change, because you are a friendly kid when you want to be."

PART VI

MISCELLANEOUS
ISSUES

16

Children's Fears

YOUNGER CHILDREN

What do you say when your three-year-old says, "There is a big monster in my room, and he's going to get me"? Many parents find themselves saying things like, "Don't be silly—there are no monsters in your room" or "You know there's nothing in your room. We told you that before, and you're driving us nuts with all that stuff!" or "You're just trying to get out of your bedroom at night!" Naturally, the kid answers back with, "Yes they *are* in my room, and they're going to get me!"

Monsters and goblins are quite real to young children, but you can feel pretty silly trying to argue with a child rationally about whether or not they exist. A child will often get more terrified of her monster thoughts the less understanding you become. Some professionals have advised parents to take the child into her bedroom to "kill the monsters" and then to put a sign on the door to tell them to keep away. Some children are helped by this, but it still conveys the idea that monsters are real and that all a child needs is power over them. In my view, young children need a sense of what is real and what is not. Monsters are not real, but children's feelings about them are real. Young children's minds are wonderously imaginative. A child who is developing creatively in many ways can suddenly see her world in a very unreal way and scare herself half to death.

This strength of imagination is apparent if you watch how a child reacts to playing "monster" with a father. Dad is chasing and mak-

153

ing noises, while the kid screams with delight. Suddenly the child becomes afraid, and Dad looks like the Incredible Hulk. Dad says, "What's wrong? It's me!" but the kid just keeps crying. When the situation gets to this point, the child's imagination is so strong that she just can't stop the feelings.

First Step

Acknowledge the child's feeling. "Boy, I can really see you're afraid of the monsters. Come over here and let me give you a hug. I'm going to help you get over your worry."

Second Step

Say, "Let's go in your room, and we'll look and I'll show you there are no monsters in there. See? We looked all over the room and down the hall, and there are no monsters. Monsters are make-believe."

Third Step

Give the child a flashlight so that she will feel more control. Walk with her from her bedroom to your room, and say, "It takes only ten seconds for me to get to your room when you're afraid. You have lots of control over your fears by knowing how fast I can come to you."

You could ask your child if she would like to see how monsters are made for the movies or how masks make people look scary on the outside when on the inside they are still real people. This also gives a child a feeling of control when she needs it.

Fourth Step

Use this step when your child has awakened during the night with fears. In the morning, say, "Gee, remember how scared you were last night, and you're OK this morning. You're always OK in the morning. The worries and scary thoughts are in your mind, and they always go away. See how strong you are? You can make the thoughts go away."

OLDER CHILDREN

Because of the complexities of modern life and the tremendous availability of information through the media, children are more aware than ever before of the possibility of harm coming to them. Most parents wish they could protect their children from exposure to frightening events. It is normal in the course of development for children to go through periods of developing fears without the "help" they get from the media. Fears of natural disasters or of parents dying are usual at this age, but added to this now are fears of kidnapping or being killed themselves. We have our hands full in helping children to not feel overwhelmed by these issues. We want to help children develop a healthy sense of self-protection without frightening them. We can do this by helping them with their feelings concerning frightening events and by giving them good information about what makes their world safe.

First Step

Be aware of what kinds of things your child worries about. Tell her that you want to help her with those worries and that you want her to come and tell you whenever she is having scary feelings. "We can talk about it, and you'll feel better."

Second Step

Check with your child periodically, once a month or so, to see if anything is worrying her, making it clear that you are available to talk about it. This is not putting thoughts into her head that are not there; it is letting your child know that you are aware of the possibility of her worrying and that you are concerned for her feelings. It is true that if you mention this kind of concern too often, say every day or week, you can make a kid bonkers and afraid of every nook and cranny in the house. You should use good judgment and caution.

Third Step

Get your child to tell you what she remembers that she is to do when she's afraid. Be very supportive. "Remember what I've told you to do when you are afraid? Now see, you can help yourself with your fears." If the child doesn't remember what you've told her, say, "I'm going to go over this with you again, because I think it will help you to not worry. But, honey, I want you to try to remember, because this will help you." This would be a good time to have a discussion about all the people in your child's world who help her feel safe and whom she can remember when she's feeling scared.

Fourth Step

Use this step if your child keeps asking about frightening things happening to her. Remember, what the child is really saying is, "I still feel worried." You can say to her, "I think you're asking about these possibilities because no matter what I tell you, it still feels scary. I understand that, but I want you to know that those scary feelings will go away—they always do. Remind yourself to say, 'Does it help me feel better when I talk about these scary things?' If it does, I will talk to you for a few minutes about them. But if that still doesn't help, you will have to remind yourself that when you keep talking about this, you just worry more. You can say to yourself, 'I have to get myself in control.' If you don't remember to do that, I'm going to tell you, because I know it's the best way for you to get over your worries."

As adults, we know that when we get scared, we have to control our thoughts and stop focusing on what scares us. If we can teach children how to do this at a young age, they will feel much more control over their fears.

17

Toileting

Have you ever heard yourself say, "If you'll only go to the toilet, I'll take you to Disneyland every day for the rest of your life"? Have you ever threatened your child with, "Live in your diapers for the rest of your life and see if I care"? If you have, then you know the agony of "toileting."

Before considering how you should deal with toilet training, this comment is for those parents who continue to keep their children in diapers: In order for your child to feel that he is a "big boy," you must be willing to keep him in training pants even if it is more work for you.

By keeping him in diapers you may be playing it safe—you will avoid finding a trail of urine or "poo poo" extending from one end of the house to the other. Unlike most trails this is one you would prefer not to follow. Also, the odor may necessitate an urgent call for gas masks. Keeping a child in diapers discourages a child from using the toilet while you are trying to train him. It is called a "mixed message."

Since there are many good books on the subject of toilet training, we will focus on the fact that sometimes toileting doesn't go smoothly and becomes a locked-in struggle attended by anxiety and anger between parent and child. Parents lose sleep, face public embarrassment, and have nightmares of their children living in diapers until they are twenty-one.

Many parents tend to feel that their children are intentionally being uncooperative and can go to the toilet any time they want. The parent's agenda is for the training to be uncomplicated. When this agenda is not met, parents frequently become upset and increase their child's anxiety.

Toileting is anxiety-provoking for parents because they have so little control. You can't make your child go to the toilet. Toileting can become a power struggle between you and your child. If he has been upset about this issue, he may not use the toilet because of the anger or fear he feels toward you. Once again, observation of agendas can unlock the struggle.

The child's basic agenda is something like this, "Why are you making me do this? Sometimes it's scary." "Who wants to sit on a silly hole anyway and drop part of my body into it?" When you think of what this whole process looks like from the child's point of view, adults end up looking pretty weird. We make the biggest fuss over dropping this funny looking mass into the toilet, and the kid sees the grown-ups smiling or even cheering because he's done such a wonderful thing. The next thing he knows, we flush it away. The kid must think we're absolutely crazy! We cheer him on for getting this out of him, we cheer him on for this stuff swirling around in the water, we make him look at it, we praise him for making "do do" and "poo poo," and together we watch it as it's flushed away. Yes, indeed, these are very weird people. If this stuff is so marvelous, why not keep it or play with it instead of throwing it away? He's confused. Sometimes he gets "positive" attention (when he drops it in the pot); yet he sometimes gets "negative" attention for the same thing (when he goes in his pants). Occasionally he's sent to the bathroom as a form of punishment, and he sits on the pot because Mommy's mad at him. And the next time, you're cheering him on when he's on the toilet. The bathroom as a place to go to the toilet can have little value to a child. He may not perceive it as a particularly wonderful place to perform an activity that has become associated with anxiety.

Many children (between two and four) find nothing wrong with the smell of their bowel movements. They feel comfortable about something that's a part of their body. Some parents who are locked in may make the child feel that there is something wrong with these feelings; their disapproval makes the child feel strange because he feels comfortable about it. He gets mixed up thinking that he's done something bad by making a mess, and he becomes increasingly anxious. Also, some parents become frustrated because when their child appears to be trained, he regresses by having a bowel movement in his pants again. This is a normal process for many children who are learning toileting. Parents have the mistaken belief that this shouldn't happen.

Some of the steps to be reminded of if you're locked in are the following.

First Step

It would be advisable to have your child checked by your pediatrician if he continues having difficulties. However, in most cases it isn't a physical problem.

Second Step

If you have continued to be frustrated and angry with your child, you need to know what to verbalize to him. You say, "You know I have been getting too mad at you when you mess in your pants. I want you to know that I love you very much, and I am sorry for being so upset. I need to help you learn to use the toilet, and I'm going to try to find a better way to do it." This is basically an apology by you for overreacting in an inappropriate manner. If you are struggling to control yourself over this issue, it is important to repeat the preceding comments. Don't assume you'll stop getting mad overnight!

Third Step

Make up a chart that provides spaces for every day of the week, and divide it into two sections. One section on the chart should be tallied for the child's willingness to cooperate, and the other section should be tallied for each time that he uses the toilet. Give him a sticker to put on the chart every day for either of these efforts. At the end of each day he should be given a reward. For example, if he likes stories he might be given an extra story at bedtime for each sticker he received. In other words, give him a small reward at the end of each day.

Children between two and three years of age sometimes need an immediate reward after using the toilet. It could be in the form of praise, a piece of candy, or something that is important to them. The chart works most effectively with children over the age of three.

Fourth Step

Set up a daily routine for your child to sit on the toilet at regular intervals so he will feel comfortable. Limit the time to two to five minutes. Tell him, "We're going to do this every day just for a little bit until you learn to use the toilet. I will stay in the bathroom while you are learning to do this." You must be consistent with this procedure if you want to reduce anxiety. The point of sitting on the toilet is to get the child used to the idea that this is his job until he learns to use the toilet on his own. Practicing sitting on the toilet helps him associate "going" on the toilet rather than in his diapers. This helps reduce anxiety for some children. If your child becomes unusually anxious about sitting on the toilet, start with the potty. It may be necessary for him to sit on the potty for only a brief time in the beginning; you can gradually increase the time.

Fifth Step

Verbally reward your child for making any effort to sit on the toilet regularly, without fussing, by saying, "Good, you're really trying, and I know you're going to learn to go to the toilet." Even if your child becomes upset while sitting on the toilet, you should encourage him by saying empathetically, "You will have to sit here for a couple of minutes, but everything is going to be OK." You must give encouragement for any effort on your child's part, no matter how slight. Even if you see only mild improvement, you should nevertheless praise him. Remember what I said earlier in the book about increments of change. Praise for the slightest change helps him to see that you're aware of his effort. It would be encouraging to say, "Well, you really have tried, even though you weren't able to use the toilet." If you encourage him and induce him to keep trying, you are likely to see some results.

Sixth Step

Tell your child that if he makes a mess in his pants, it's his job to help Mom or Dad clean it up. Even if he's very small, you can have him carry what he has messed in to the hamper or wastecan. This way he learns that it is his responsibility, the same as it would be if he has spilled a glass of milk. Sharing the cleaning job is much better than you magically taking care of it as if he had nothing to do with it. Even for the youngest child, being taught to help teaches him to associate having a bowel movement with the beginning of responsibility.

Seventh Step

You must remember that all children eventually learn to go to the toilet no matter what we do. If you reduce your own anxiety, you won't make your child feel that he's doing something wrong. I know that it's frustrating, but it will be worth it to give it a try. If you try all of these suggestions and they do not work, the only way to unlock this struggle is to accept the idea that your child will go to the toilet when he is ready, if you don't continue to be part of the problem. Eventually, your acceptance of his struggle will aid in his maturing. He will learn to use the toilet.

DAY WETTING

Sometimes, by peeking out of the window while your child plays outside, you know he is just about to have trouble. You notice him jumping up and down, moving his legs crisscross and back and forth. He's in the process of a major decision. Should he stop and go to the dumb toilet, or just keep playing, hoping that the jumping will control the urge to urinate? As we know, this just doesn't work.

One of the funniest questions in the world is, "Johnny, do you have to go to the bathroom?" As he grabs himself and furiously says, "No!" and then proceeds to wet all over himself, you say the famous, "I told you so!" You also make statements to your child like, "Why can't you remember to go to the toilet?" In turn, he says, "Well, I wasn't sure," or "I didn't have to go that badly." Then you say, "Well, you better remember the next time."

The reason day wetters wait until the last minute to go to the bathroom is because they tend to be the type who play very actively and who are very involved. They hate to stop what they're doing. Anxiety is not usually the cause, although it can be part of it. This is the child who gets so involved that the choice between peeing in his pants and stopping a game is no contest. Peeing wins eight out of ten times.

So, you have talked to the kid until you are blue in the face. He promises that he'll go to the toilet the next time, but he doesn't. His agenda is to keep playing and at the same time stop the urine from coming out. Well, folks, that doesn't work. But he hates to interrupt his activity, and that's why he tells you he doesn't have to go as he's frantically jumping up and down grabbing himself.

Now, parents don't panic. Deal with this in the following way.

First Step

Let him know in a supportive way that he's having a problem of being aware when he has to urinate while he's playing. You want to help him become aware of when he needs to go to the toilet. Every half hour he will have to stop what he's doing and go into the bathroom, until he learns to pay better attention to his need to urinate.

Being a good observer means noticing when this is likely to occur. You will usually find that during the day it's in the midst of a period when he's playing vigorously. If it's from the time he gets out of school until dinner, he will learn that unless he controls himself, you will interfere with his pleasure. And a kid hates that! In this way, you are making him pay attention to the fact that his enjoyment will be curtailed unless he takes care of the business of going to the bathroom.

Second Step

Your child should be responsible for all of the practical tasks involved when he wets, like putting his clothes in the proper place and cleaning himself. Until these tasks are finished, he can't go back out to play. If he's a younger child, you may have to help him with some of it.

Once you set up this structure, you no longer have to ask him if he has to go to the bathroom. Just remind him that he has to use the toilet instead of urinating on himself so he can develop control. Eventually, when your child realizes you're going to stick to the routine, he will catch himself and go to the toilet before you interfere with his play. If you keep this up long enough, you will be able to stop asking all of those questions like, "Do you have to go?" or, "Why are you holding yourself?"

NIGHT WETTING

"Don't you know I have only one more clean sheet?" or, "Why are you doing this now, of all times?" If your child is a night wetter, you instantly recognize these statements as the frustrated exclamations of a parent who has been called from his bed at 3:00 A.M.

Your child's reactions to night wetting might vary greatly. Some children will actually not be bothered by it, which drives many parents crazy. Other children are quite sensitive to it, and get up to let you know that they are wet and need help. Some children sleep through the night even though they're wet, because they're very deep sleepers. They don't seem to be aware of it.

First we have to recognize that in terms of normal development, there are many possible reasons that a child lacks self-control. It can sometimes be normal for wetting to be an expression of a child's anxiety. Usually when the anxiety is reduced, the child will achieve self-control. Many times the anxiety is not related to the issue of wetting or a bowel movement, but to a seemingly unrelated problem. Of course, four- or five-year-olds cannot turn to you and say, "I figured out why I'm wetting. I've noticed that you and Dad aren't getting along, and I am wetting because I am trying to tell both of you to stop fighting." Your five-year-old has no way to tell you that his wetting may be an expression of his anxiety.

Be careful not to perpetuate the problem. Some parents get so upset about the issue of control that they actually cause the anxiety in their child. I know that it's no fun getting up in the middle of the night to run around carrying dirty sheets while your spouse is still sleeping. But the commotion you generate is a major factor in your child's wetting problem.

So, what do you do about night wetting? I suppose you're thinking, "This guy is going to tell me all of the things that my grandmother told me. What I want is a magical solution." I'm simply going to remind you of the basic procedures that sometimes help. You will probably have to live through an inconvenient period before this problem is solved.

First Step

Tell your child that you are going to stop getting mad because he's wetting the bed at night. (This, by the way, is one of the many Academy Award–winning performances you'll give after reading this book.) Tell him, "I know you don't want to wet yourself, and I need to learn a better way to help you. I'm going to set some new rules to help you learn how to control yourself. From now on when you wake up, I'll help you change, but you must help, too, because it's your job to help clean up. You're big enough to help yourself with this problem, too." Continue by saying, "Every time you can control yourself at night, I will give you a small reward for the times you can stay dry. You don't have to worry. There will be no more punishment, because I realize that I've been wrong. If you're wet, you're wet. I know you are not trying to do this on purpose." By saying this, you are telling your child that you're taking some responsibility for the way you've been locked in and that you really want to help.

Second Step

By being matter-of-fact and by having your child take part in the process, you're telling him he has made a mistake. It's not a bad mistake, but he has to learn to be responsible for it. Even if he walks bleary-eyed, carrying clothing to put in the hamper, you're beginning to teach him that he will also be inconvenienced. If you always take care of everything, the kid may wait until he's twenty-one before he realizes that it's not your responsibility. If you don't make him responsible, he will learn that everything will always be taken care of for him, so what's the big deal?

If your child is able to sleep through the night after wetting, without being bothered by a soaked bed, follow the same procedure in the morning.

Third Step

Control liquids. If your child is having trouble with this, have a specific time to drink liquids, preferably one hour before bedtime. (There's nothing new about this suggestion.)

Fourth Step

Prepare your child ahead of time in a positive way by setting up a reward chart that he can keep in his room. This is particularly helpful for children between the ages of four and nine. The chart will not have a negative effect. It rewards your child for the days he wakes up dry. You should also discuss with him what small reward he would like for staying dry. (This does not include a new Cadillac or a trip to Acapulco.) It might be his favorite gum or a small toy. You don't want him to think that everything he does should be associated with some huge reward.

If you treat the subject of wetting in a matter-of-fact way, and you reinforce the fact that your child helped himself, you are telling him that you are confident he can gain control. You're saying that you are not worried about it, and it's OK if he's having trouble, but everything will be all right!

Sometimes, as a parent, you may not feel that it is going to be all right. In fact, you might feel that your child is ruining your life. But he wants to resolve this as much as you do, and eventually, it *will* be resolved. If you continue to act angry, you will only increase your child's anxiety, and you will probably make it more difficult for him to control his night wetting.

18

Kids Who Won't Listen

Have you ever, in exasperation, found yourself yelling the following things to your child: "Do you have wax in your ears?" "Are you deaf?" "I just called you, and you never act like you hear me. I tell you to do things, and you just stare at me." Or, do you repeat the famous command, "Now repeat what I just told you to do"? Parents who feel that they have very little control usually try to get their children to listen to them in this manner. But none of this yelling changes the child's behavior.

Parents have the mistaken idea that their request should have magical power, so that when they tell their child to do something, she should listen. This is another example of a parent's agenda that differs from that of a child. A child's agenda is to pay no attention to you because she is doing basically what she wants to do, which is enjoying herself.

Parents who are not observant often yell needlessly at their kids. Mom yells out from another room, "Get in here for dinner," and, "Did you clean up your room?" The child doesn't respond or else she says, "In a minute." She doesn't move. Basically, she has learned that she doesn't have to listen.

The real issue is how to hold a child's attention when she doesn't want to listen. She doesn't want to listen to you because you will either lecture her or let her know you are angry. Remember, a child's agenda is to do what she wants; your agenda is to make her listen to you without resistance. Children tune out because they get tired of all the words; they know that most of the time the hollering adds up to nothing more than hot air. Here are some steps to try to change this locked-in pattern.

First Step

Mom tells her child, "I haven't done a good job of telling you that you must listen to me. I yell too much, and I tell you the same things over and over. From now on there will be a new rule. You will not say, 'Just a minute' or 'I'm in the middle of something.' There will be no more acting like you don't hear me. I'm not saying this because I'm mad at you, but because it's time that you learn you have to do things when Mom asks you to do them."

Second Step

"When I ask you to do something, I'll give you five minutes before it has to be done. I'll give you a warning, and this will give you a chance to think about what Mom has requested." If that doesn't help, go on to the third step.

Third Step

You must say, "When I ask you to do something, I will ask you only once. If you don't listen, I'm going to stop you from whatever you are doing and make you finish what I have asked you to do." This means physically getting up and seeing that your child does it. You are showing her that you can make her do it.

Fourth Step

"If these rules haven't helped you to listen better, then I will have to interrupt whatever you are doing until you can learn to listen. If you continue to make me get up to force you to do what is expected, which I will do, you will lose the privilege of going back to your activity for the entire evening. I hope you can learn to follow these rules, so you won't lose some of your own time."

19

The Famous "Why" Question

Why do parents have an insatiable need to constantly ask their kids "why" they don't do what they want them to do? The reason is that they have the mistaken belief that their children really know the reason why. If you listen to yourself, you'll hear yourself asking your child wonderful questions like the following: "Why did you do that?" when your four-year-old child pushes his dog into the swimming pool. Your child's inevitable response is, of course, "because." Your next move is to say, "That's no answer," and he looks dumbfounded, silly, or guilty. Meanwhile the dog is drowning in the pool while you're still trying to find out "why."

If your child is eight years old, the same scene might go like this: "Why did you push the puppy in the pool?" His answer is, "Because he brushed by me and he got hair on me." "That's no reason to push him into the pool!" you shout. "Why did you do it? I can't believe you did that!" A child this age then says, "I didn't mean to. I . . . it was an . . . an accident!"

Other famous "whys" include, "Why do I have to tell you not to scratch yourself in front of visitors?" "Why do I have to tell you twenty times to pick up your toys?" They go on and on. With few exceptions, I've yet to find a parent who gets a satisfactory answer to such questions.

In addition to "because," and, "I don't know," children come up with other interesting responses. The one that really infuriates parents is: "Because I felt like it." This causes high blood pressure, along with the famous blue-in-the-face or storm trooper reaction, possibly accompanied by the cold shoulder response.

168

The question is, why does the "why" question frustrate parents so much, and why can't children understand the "why" question? If you don't know why now, read on. I know by this time I had better be able to come up with a good answer or I'm in serious trouble.

For starters, the "why" question is meaningless. Aha! You have learned something already. Now, what is your agenda as a parent in asking the "why" question? You want your child to come up with some brilliant interpretation of his motives. You are still waiting for the day when your four-year-old comes in and says, "Mommy, I'm bad. I shouldn't have done it. I learned my lesson, though." Of course, the day your child does this, you'll probably have a heart attack right on the spot. And they'll carry you away forever if you actually hear your eight-year-old say, "I pushed the dog in the pool because you made me so mad two hours ago. I was taking my hostility out on the animal."

You may be thinking, "This author is crazy. I'm not asking my kid to understand all that." Maybe you aren't in so many words, but it's the one thing you want when you ask the "why" question. You also want him to admit that he did something wrong. But asking him why he did it is an indirect attempt to get an admission of wrongdoing from him. You think that if you ask your child why he did something, he'll learn something from it. This is not the case.

First Step

Begin to take more appropriate action by saying, "You know that it's not acceptable to throw the dog into the pool." Then, if necessary, follow through with a meaningful consequence like an early bedtime or the loss of television time. If you ask your child, "Why?" he doesn't know what you're really asking him. He isn't quite sure what you want, and most of all, he's going to try to minimize it as much as possible. He has learned that "why" questions are only asked when he's in trouble.

As a mode of observing your own behavior, ask yourself why you're asking why, and what it is you really want from your child. If you do this, I guarantee—without any money back, of course—that you will be asking why much less. More often you'll be telling your child specifically what is unacceptable behavior, and what is going to happen if he repeats that action.

The "why" question stems from exasperation. When you see that your child is repeating a behavior over and over again when you've already spoken to him about it, you feel helpless. Specific expectations and consequences will make you feel more effective.

Second Step

Think about what you want from your child rather than asking him why. Look at what he did that you found unacceptable, let him know how you feel about it, and tell him what the consequence will be the next time this behavior occurs. Or, if he rarely displays this behavior, let him know that you didn't like what he did, but since he usually doesn't do this, simply tell him to remember not to do it again.

Think about some of the things we've discussed earlier in this book about expectations, consequences, and follow-through. If you can have clear communication and appropriate consequences, you may find yourself making progress with your child.

PART VII
LOOSE ENDS

20

Weird "Normal"
Behavior

During my lectures and seminars on parenting, I frequently hear questions that fall into two general categories: "Why does my kid act so weird?" and "Will my child grow up to be a normal adult?" Parents are always concerned about normal development behaviors that seem abnormal to them. Kids have interesting ways of telling us what they want us to know. Although their behaviors may make very little sense to adults, they are unique and effective ways for children to handle events in their own world and to get their messages across to us concerning their unusual reactions to situations or to us. Here are some examples of normal behavior that can seem very abnormal to parents.

One family came into therapy because their four-year-old was collecting bags of trash and keeping them in his room. At first the parents thought this was funny, but after the thirteenth bag of trash, they wondered if he needed to be put away or if they did. When they told their son that he didn't need all this trash, he insisted he did need it. I asked the parents if they had ever told the child that he couldn't have the trash in his room. They said that they hadn't because they didn't want him to get upset. I told them that they needed to tell their son that he could no longer put trash in his room. I warned them that he would probably have a big tantrum and tell them he'd die without his trash. He did have the tantrum, but in three days he was still alive and over his trash-collecting phase, and things were back to normal in the household.

Little children around the age of four become very involved in hoarding objects of various kinds. This little boy found collecting trash to be pleasurable, important, and meaningful. However weird it seemed to his parents, it is an example of a normal behavior for his age.

In another family a brilliant ten-year-old announced to his parents that he no longer felt it was necessary to do homework. This was a child who always did extremely well in school and had never given his parents any reason to worry about his ability to achieve. Now suddenly he announced that homework wasn't important, that he could get A's without it. The parents went bonkers, and a power struggle was born. This was not merely the challenge to parental authority that it appeared to be. The boy was trying to evaluate for himself the importance of homework. He felt proud of himself for being able to get good grades without doing homework, and he wanted to test his parents' reaction to this fact. Does anyone ever tell a kid that from the age of five to eighteen he's going to be doing homework every night? These parents thought their child was becoming rebellious, that he would never study again, and that he would probably lose interest in school altogether. His reaction to homework was actually very normal, but his way of expressing it was sophisticated and unusual for his age.

Another family came to see me because they were worried about their six-year-old boy. He liked to play "dress up," and he played with dolls more than with "boy's toys." At school he preferred to play with the girls. His parents had begun to argue about all this, the father saying, "You're making a sissy out of him," and the mother saying, "If you'd spend more time with him instead of going bowling, maybe he'd like to do the things you like." The father said helpful things to his son like, "What are the other boys going to think if they see you playing with dolls? They're going to make fun of you unless you stop." Mother tried to help by saying, "Leave the boy alone. It doesn't hurt anything. He's just a little boy."

As you can see, this issue created great marital harmony. At this point, they sought my help. They were both wondering if their son would grow up to be normal. Normal meant doing things that are "boylike." They had already tried to change him in various ways. They put him in a T-ball league, but when he swung and missed the ball, he didn't seem to care. In the outfield he was one of those kids who would pick flowers and not see the ball when it came toward him. It drove his father nuts! They continued to encourage him to take part in other typical "masculine" activities, hoping to make him develop that part of himself. They also talked about all this a great deal in the family, so much so that the little boy began getting angry whenever a discussion like this would start.

As I began to talk with the parents about their son, some important ideas about the different ways children grow were clarified. I emphasized that as parents, we need to accept differences in our children, no matter how much they go against the grain of our thinking. By the time they came to me, they had made their kid feel that he was just plain weird, if he hadn't been feeling that way already. When I helped them look at this child carefully, they saw that he was a very creative boy in many ways. He could draw with great imagination, was interested in books, and even acted out fantasy like a budding actor.

The important issue for these parents was to see how their child differed from their expectations and to accept these differences as normal. Their boy was never going to be a jock, throwing the ball around with Dad and making diving catches in the outfield. But he would grow up to be a sensitive, wonderful person.

This story shows how parents can sometimes act as weird as they think their kid is acting when they try to force attributes on him that are not natural. The important point to remember is that children have different temperaments and grow up in different ways, and can still come out just fine as adults.

In a somewhat similar situation, a family came to therapy with an aggressive little five-year-old "tomboy." She had been going around the house telling her mother that girls were dumb and that men were smarter and had more fun. She didn't like any of the girls at school and called them "silly." She would wear only pants and played football and "boys games." This child's mother was an attractive, feminine woman who couldn't figure out how she had gotten a daughter who wouldn't wear dresses. No other women in the family were like this. The little girl was an "alien" to her mother. The father wasn't too worried; he just said she'd grow out of it.

As I talked with this family, it became clear that they rarely spent time with their daughter. Mother was very competent and very busy taking care of her child's functional needs with efficiency.

Father worked all the time and just wasn't around the house much. As we explored the family structure, it became evident that there was one special person who influenced the daughter's activities. An uncle kept company with her quite a lot, playing football with her and taking her many places. He absolutely enjoyed this child, and she responded by developing her strongest emotional attachment to him. She thought everything he did was wonderful, and she tried to emulate him in many ways, including his clothes.

Once I got the parents to actively involve themselves in their daughter's life, she stopped saying she didn't like "girl things" and started copying her mother in small ways. She now liked to do things with her mother and father, and still had fun with her uncle, too.

Both stories illustrate the importance of accepting children when they're different than what we'd hoped for. Both these children's behaviors were very normal for who they were. The little girl's behavior showed her parents that some of her needs were not being met, despite her mother's competence. In both families the parents were seeing the children's behavior as weird and strange, rather than as different or as an attempt to tell them something about their lives.

Then there is the story of a four-year-old boy who had not acknowledged the birth of his sister, who was two when the family came to therapy. This little fellow had never referred to her by name, always calling her "it" or "thing." The whole family had made a fuss about the coming of a second child—how happy they would all be and how great it would be for the little boy to be a big brother. From the time his mother announced her pregnancy, he showed no interest. When relatives asked him about the coming event, he said, "I don't want to be a big brother." His Dad said, "You shouldn't talk like that," and his mother said, "You don't mean that." After the birth of his sister, his grandfather told him, "You're so lucky to have a little sister. Isn't she beautiful?" "She's ugly," was his reply. He even told anyone who asked that there were three people in his family: his father, mother, and him.

These parents would have given anything just to have their son use his sister's name once. He would walk by her, bump her lightly, flick his fingers at her, and then never admit he did those things. His parents were going crazy. They wanted to know if their kid had something wrong with his eyes and couldn't see, if he was seriously disturbed, or if he was just a mean, bratty kid. I told them it was none of the above, and that they'd flunked the test!

In the course of the therapy that followed, I helped these parents see that this little boy had never been given the right to have negative feelings about how hard it is to have a little sister come into your life. For two years before the "blessed event," he had been the special child, and then suddenly everyone was fussing about the baby. He missed getting attention from his parents, and the one way he could show his anger was to deny this kid's existence. He also got attention that way, even though it was negative. He was trying to tell his parents that this was just not a magical time for him, that he was having a hard time adjusting. Even though he handled his jealousy in an off-the-wall way, his feelings were normal and understandable.

In a situation of a different sort, a family came to me because they had this marvelous, wonderful, brilliant seven-year-old child with one absolutely maddening behavior. This kid had an IQ in the upper stratosphere, but she also had an opinion on everything and advice for everyone in the family and anyone else who would listen. She advised her mother about the clothes she wore and whether or not they were color coordinated. The problem was, she was right a lot of the time! She told her father his clothes were out of style and her brother that he acted immature and that she was embarrassed to be seen with him. When this little girl heard discussions going on among adults, she would pipe up with her own opinions. If her parents got angry at her, she said, "I don't think it's necessary to talk to me in that tone of voice."

When her father gave her lecture No. 31, she would say, "Don't you remember, you've given me this same talk since I was four years old?"

This child felt there was nothing she should not know, and she was offended if adults told her she was too young to understand something. Her parents came to me feeling almost embarrassed to be complaining about this great kid. "We have this marvelous child who is absolutely driving us nuts with her unsolicited opinions about life." They wondered what they'd done wrong to create this wonderful monster.

This family had a normal little girl who'd been treated like an adult from the moment she could walk. When she was younger, her parents were delighted to watch how her mind worked, and how quickly she could learn and how well she communicated. However, what they'd done was to give her too much permission for expression, and she had developed no sense of boundaries between herself and adults. Her parents were afraid to come down too hard on her because they didn't want to squelch her wonderful spontaneity and brightness.

As with the other children I've talked about, her behavior had her parents saying to themselves, "What in the heck is wrong with this kid? Where did she get this strange way of relating to us?" However, there was nothing abnormal about her, she had just developed some extreme behavior as a result of too much permission. She was so delightful and surprising when she gave her opinions that the response she got from adults reinforced the very behavior they objected to! When her parents understood how this pattern had taken hold, they were able to put limits on her opinions and comments, and soon the family got back to normal.

It is important to try to understand what children are trying to say to us with their sometimes unusual behavior. They are constantly trying to communicate to us as they go through the normal phases of development. Remember, they do grow up to be people, just like you and I did. If you feel good about yourself in life, your children have a good chance of turning out OK, no matter what strange behavior they exhibit during their preadolescent years.

21

Questions Most Commonly Asked by Parents

Q. **If my child is behaving badly when he's four, how will he act when he's older?**

A. Sometimes children go through a "monster" phase. They fuss over everything, they don't know what they want, and they act like you're ruining their life (this feeling might be mutual). At a time like this, it's natural for a parent to project into the future and to think that his child will be totally impossible in ten years. Don't panic! Remember, as adults we get just as fussy and act just as weird as kids sometimes do.

A child's behavior at one stage of development does not always imply that particular behavior at another stage. If you learn to handle a child's attitude and behavior in effective ways now, even when he or she goes bonkers, you'll be able to help him and yourself through it.

Q. **Why are some children so difficult, no matter what you try to do to help them?**

A. This is the kid I call "the alien child," the one who comes into your family and is very different. Many parents who talk about children who are difficult are really talking about a child who is just very different from them. Nothing seems to work with this child. He or she may be very different than you in temperament, ways of doing things, and in what he wants. Perhaps you are an active, outgoing person, and you have a child who finds it uncomfortable to try new things. This child just doesn't experience the world the way you do. His behavior may create a struggle in you to accept

179

your child's differences. Another example is the father who fanta-
sizes about having a son he can teach to play ball and take to
sporting events. The little guy turns out to be very creative, soft,
and loving, and doesn't like to get hurt. This little boy will never
be a "bad dude."

A parent with this kind of challenge needs to accept the child
and love his differences. You need to evaluate whether or not the
child is doing well in the world, even though he functions so differently than you. Many children who seem "alien" are really wonderful people to parent, even though you may feel some sadness
that they can't experience the world in the same way you do.

**Q. Why does my child seem fine for months at a time, and
then go off the wall for a week or two?**
A. First, growth in a child is quite variable, and that means you're
going to see inconsistent patterns. Sometimes children use their
behaviors and attitudes to show us that they're struggling. They're
not able to directly express their feelings or to clearly understand
what is creating their discomforts. It's important, again, to think
about adult behavior. How many adults can express their feelings
openly and caringly when they're upset? Sometimes we expect kids
to do what we can't.

It is important to remember not to regress along with your child.
A child who is struggling needs understanding and consistency.
Sometimes it can help so much for a child to hear a parent say, "I
know you've been having a hard time, because you seem to be
upset a lot lately. I want you to know that we all feel that way
sometimes. Mom and Dad do. We always get over it, and so will
you."

Q. Why is parenting so difficult?
A. When was the last time you were thrown into a job with no
education or training for it, with the assumption that you should
be competent? What job do you know that changes from moment
to moment? In what job does the mood change from loving to
chaotic within one hour? What job creates such strong feelings in
you because you care so much about it? Any other job like this
you'd quit in a week! Yet, despite all this, the deep love parents
feel for their children enables them to do the hardest of parenting

tasks with great dedication and effort. Most parents see it as a monumental job but also as tremendously rewarding.

Q. Sometimes I feel as though I really don't like my kids, and it makes me feel terrible. Are these thoughts unusual?

A. When a parent has these thoughts it is usually because of feeling frustrated and upset with something in his life or in the parenting experience. It is rare to hear parents talk about just "not liking" their child. Parents who have these feelings are not recognizing that they just don't like coping with their child at that particular moment and are finding the task of parenting overwhelming.

Whenever we are intimately involved with another human being, our deepest feelings are evoked. And what could be more intimate than our feelings for our child? These feelings include love, pain, fear, and sometimes even rejection. The important thing to remember is to not be afraid of these feelings, because if you have a healthy, loving relationship with your offspring, the negative aspect of any feeling will pass fairly quickly. If these feelings have become noticeable to your child, or if you have told him out of anger that you don't like him or her, you can make things better by talking about it. "Once in a while I may act like I don't like you, but that's only because I'm feeling upset. I want you to remember that, even when I'm upset, my loving feelings are so much stronger that they always overpower my upset feelings."

Q. Why does it seem that my children are intentionally trying to upset me?

A. It is important to learn that until children are almost into adolescence, they don't have the kind of calculating feelings that adults have. It is only as we get older that we develop the kind of sophisticated understanding of what hurts and upsets others. If we grow up in a relatively healthy way, we don't exercise this ability to hurt others very often.

Children behave in a variety of complex ways in their attempt to understand and master their world. They're going to express these feelings to their parents in very personal ways. However, they rarely try to get back at their parents. They don't realize that they are causing hurt feelings; what they are doing is demonstrating their dissatisfaction at not getting their way. As a parent you need to try very hard not to personalize your child's behavior toward you. If you do this, you will make your child too responsible for your emotions. Young children need to experience a parent who can handle whatever feeling a child feels, however hurtful.

Q. How should I handle it when I'm notified that my child is having a problem in school?

A. Your first reactions are probably to imagine the world has come to an end, that the child's school life is doomed, and that you have a major problem on your hands. Even if your reactions aren't that major, it's normal for school problems to create worry in a parent.

Teachers will react well to you if you try to respond to the problem in the following way. "Whatever the issues are with our child, we are very interested in talking with you to understand it and in working together." This will create a rapport. When this cooperative tone is established, ask the following questions. What are some specific examples of the child's problem, and how has the teacher tried to deal with it so far? Does the teacher have specific suggestions about what you can to do to help?

If you are not comfortable with the suggestions given, tell her you would like to get a second opinion and get back to her for more discussion. You are not doing this to be disagreeable or obstinate, but to do your best to help your child.

You will find that if you approach a teacher in this manner, you are likely to get a positive response.

Q. My child only behaves well about half the time, and that doesn't seem like enough to me.

A. Those parents who have an easy-to-raise kid can forget this question! As parents, we often have a wonderful "Father Knows Best" fantasy that kids should behave most of the time—otherwise something is wrong.

There are children who have easygoing temperaments and who mind all the time. There are also children who behave out of fear and intimidation. In my opinion, the latter behavior is the result of an overuse of parental power. My feeling is that if you have a child who behaves about 60 percent of the time, you and your child are doing fine. How many adults do you know who behave well and do what you want them to do more than 60 percent of the time? Does your spouse respond to your requests 60 percent of the time? Your friends? Your close relatives? It's a funny paradox. We have higher behavioral standards for little kids who know less about the world than we do for adults. And often the adults don't do as well as the kids!

You need to understand that one of the tasks of childhood is to test the limits of the world. This means that kids are going to be pushing for their needs a great deal of the time. And that translates to mean that problem behavior is a very normal part of parenting.

There is no doubt that effective parenting techniques can improve your child's behavior. At the same time, you need to have realistic expectations for your children and not get upset at them for acting like the kids they are.

Q. Why does my child listen to my husband, even though they don't spend as much time together?

A. Most mothers who ask this question at seminars show an appropriate degree of exasperation and frustration. Their husbands often seem to be saying (a little smugly), "Well, they're no problem for *me.*"

Many mothers have the ongoing fantasy that they'd like their husbands to trade places with them and see how they felt after fourteen hours a day with the kids.

Family roles have changed rapidly in the past decade because of women working outside the home, but certain aspects of these roles are evolving more slowly. A mother's role with young children still tends to be that of the nurturer and the one who concerns herself with children's feelings, worries, and anxieties. In many families, the father's role is still that of the person who represents the world outside the home and who is the authority figure. Children see him differently than they do their mother.

Men generally talk with an easier sense of authority because that has been their role in the world. Children tend to respond and listen to this kind of voice, rather than a nurturant voice, when discipline is needed. Parents who are observant of their own behavior will be aware of when an authority voice is needed as opposed to a nurturant one.

The parent who is primary caretaker tends to get the best and the worst of children. Children get very comfortable in expressing a wide range of feelings with the parent they are with the most. They also get used to that parent's personality. For example, when this parent goes bonkers, her child probably knows just when she'll recover and become loving again. Children know that difficulties with Mom tend to get resolved. They've learned her patterns from spending so much time with her.

Children also tend to show their regressive side more easily to the nurturing parent. They want more, as if to say, "You're the one who's supposed to take care of all my needs forever."

Sometimes fathers are seen by their children as vague figures who are in the house a limited time, who talk and play less but make lots of rules. Until a child gets older, he doesn't know how his father's personality "works" like he does his mother's. He is less likely to know what happens when Dad gets mad or how he works through problems. Also, in an effort to please this less-present parent, a child may go out of his way to stay in control. As a child gets older and comes to know Dad better, the child will generally "test" him more. By learning to use the material in this book, a parent of either gender can become the loving authority children need.

Q. What are some simple rules a parent should consider to protect children from current problems, such as molestation?

A. Using the concept of being a good observer, parents can protect children from harm by an awareness of the people in their lives. We should know as much as possible about our children's caretakers, including family members. Parents should be alert to any changes in a child's behavior when the child has been around a particular adult. Behavior changes to concern yourself with are overanxiousness, unhappiness, or signs of uncomfortableness. It's important to remember that I'm not saying these behaviors are always signs that something serious has happened. By noticing such behavior changes, you are becoming aware of the subtle ways children show they're uncomfortable. You can speak to your child to give him a sense of your awareness and to let him know he can rely on you for help if it's needed.

"You seemed worried and quiet when we came home from the baby-sitter. Did anything happen to upset you?"

If the child says yes, praise him for being able to tell you. If he says no, say, "I'm going to talk to the baby-sitter because I want to make sure everything is OK."

In front of the child and in a nonaccusatory way, you can say the following to the adult: "Jimmy was upset the morning after he'd spent time with you. Did anything happen that he had a problem with?"

This sends the message to your child that he is always able to tell you when he is upset and that you will always be there to protect him. It also demonstrates that it is safe to talk about problems in front of other people. By doing this you are saying to your child, "I am very concerned about any struggle you're having. All of your feelings concern me. You can count on me because I love you."

The suggested reading list at the end of this book includes books on this subject.

Conclusion

By teaching appropriate behavior with an attitude that conveys loving and caring, parents can have a profound effect on their children and can help them to cope more effectively with the problems they will have to face while trying to develop into mature human beings.

Parenting is hard work, the hardest job that anyone can ever have. Improving a child's behavior is as important as providing shelter, clothing, and education. Most parents do it as it occurs, not as a policy of daily work with the child.

Many parents become threatened when they see regressive behavior. They think, "Oh, this isn't working," so they run out and get another book—and turn in the last three books. This is understandable when you're frustrated. Hopefully, what you've learned by reading this book is to refocus on your own behavior. At what point was *your* attitude inappropriate or the consequence you chose unsuitable? Have you fallen back into your old trap?

There are times when parents feel irritable or confused. Children feel the same way.

As you learn not to become locked into your child's behavior and become more sensitive to your child's feelings, you will develop a better understanding of the motives for his behavior. This will help prevent you from too often making regressive remarks like, "Get that snotty look off your face." This clarification should help you to have a deeper understanding and a closer relationship with your child.

Suggested Reading List

General Development

Child Behavior, by Frances L. Ilg et al. New York: Harper and Row, 1981.

Mr. Mom: A Guide to Baby and Child Care, by Mary Ann Neifert M.D. New York: G. P. Putnam's Sons, 1986.

The First Three Years of Life, by Burton L. White. New York: Prentice Hall Press, 1985.

How to Parent, by Fitzhugh Dodson. New York: New American Library, 1973.

Infants and Mothers, by T. Berry Brazelton. New York: Dell Publishing, 1983.

On Becoming a Family, by T. Berry Brazelton. New York: Dell Publishing, 1981.

Toddlers and Parents, by T. Berry Brazelton. New York: Dell Publishing, 1976.

Emotional Development

How to Discipline with Love, by Fitzhugh Dodson. New York: New American Library, 1978.

How to Talk So Kids Will Listen and Listen So Kids Will Talk, by Adele Faber and Elaine Mazlish. New York: Avon Books, 1982.

The Magic Years, by Selma H. Fraiberg. New York: Charles Scribner's Sons, 1984.

Raising Good Children, by Thomas Lickona. New York: Bantam Books, 1985.

Special Concerns

The Father's Almanac, by S. Adams Sullivan. New York: Doubleday, 1986.

The Gifted Kids Survival Guide: (For Ages Ten and Under), by Judy Galbraith. Minneapolis: Free Spirit Publishing Co., 1984.

The Hurried Child: Growing Up Too Fast Too Soon, by David Elkind. Menlo Park, Calif.: Addison Wesley, 1981.

No Easy Answers: The Learning Disabled Child at Home and School, by Sally L. Smith. New York: Bantam Books, 1981.

Parents Guide to Raising a Gifted Child, by the Gifted Children Newsletter Staff and James Alvino. Boston: Little, Brown, 1984.

Something's Wrong with My Child: A Parent's Handbook About Children with Learning Disabilities, by Milton Brutten Ph. D., Charles Mangel, and Sylvia O. Richardson M.D. New York: Harcourt Brace Jovanovich, 1979.

Books on Safety for Children

The Berenstain Bears Learn About Strangers, by Stan and Jan Berenstain. New York: Random House, 1985.

It's OK To Say No, by Anne Barr. New York: Grosset and Dunlap, RGA Publishing, 1986.

No More Secrets for Me, by Oralee Wachter. Boston: Little, Brown, 1984.

You Can Say "No," by Betty Boegehold, Racine, Wis.: Western Publishing, 1985.

Books on Safety for Parents

The Safe Child Book, by Sherry K. Kraizer. New York: Dell Publishing, 1985.

Index

About the Authors

Dr. Don Fleming, a native of Los Angeles, California, has over thirty years experience in working with children and their parents. At present he is a Licensed Clinical Social Worker, and he has a Ph.D. in psychology. He is director of training at the Julia Ann Singer Center in Los Angeles. In addition to his private practice, he is a consultant lecturer for the Southern California Association of the Education of Young Children, and he is on the faculty of the Stephen Wise Temple Parenting Center in Los Angeles.

Don's strong background in working with children has made him one of the most sought after speakers on the subject in Southern California. His unique style is practical, down-to-earth, and humorous. His current speaking engagements cover a broad range of topics, from "Parenting Issues on Children," and "The Emotionally Handicapped Child," to "The Media, Television, and Its Effects on Children."

He has been a guest on numerous television and radio programs, and is currently writing two more books.

Linda Balahoutis, a free-lance writer who lives in Los Angeles, has a special interest in children's books.